Introduction

Philip Royle was born in 1950. He grew up in Lancashire and now lives in Manchester. He has been writing poetry for over twenty years and this is his first book of poems.

This selection of poems teases your thoughts, make you smile, and touches on the romantic side of life. You will find that this book is different from the norm and on occasions explains how life's experiences and the process of thought, found its way into verse.

The depth and variety of these poems will have something for everyone to enjoy. Get to know the poems, slowly read them over and ponder what's written. Most of all relax and enjoy where they take you.

Published by Phil Royle.
email: philroyle1@live.co.uk

GW00501387

To Catherine all the very best from Phil Royle.

Contents

Acknowledgemenets

To Janet

For believing

To Christian

My Inspiration

The Poet

So what kind of a person writes poetry?

What inspires a person to write and describe their feelings?

I was pondering these thoughts and decided that the only way I could explain it to others, was to describe how it felt to me.

Poets require passion and sensitive feelings
Of life's experiences and all its dealings
Love, happiness, pain and sorrow
To understand today and want tomorrow

It's not enough to feel the mood
Something inside gets stirred and moved
Like listening to music or being able to sing
Poets write; the release is everything

An orchestration of words, arranged and played
Strung together and then conveyed
To eyes and ears in sentence and verse
Dwelled on and read, for better or worse.

The Yo Yo's

My son and his school friends formed a girl, boy band when they were 8 years old. They practiced every play time and spare moment they had. They even performed for us at my Halloween party. They called themselves the Yo Yo's and inspired this poem:

The Yo Yo's are a girl, boy band
Who formed a group whilst at St Anne's
Christian, Alex, Jade and Leah
Perform for everyone who wants to hear

They rehearse their songs in and out of school
Perfecting their act which is really cool
Each has a song, with a unique routine
They are 8 years old and a mean machine

Their songs are: 'Best of both worlds 'and 'Camp rock'
'American boy' and 'Sucking too hard on a lolly pop'
They have lots of ideas and songs galore
All written and performed by the four

Mind's Eye

*I awoke one morning with the contents of a dream
still fresh in my mind. I lay there for a while, thinking
how real the dream world can appear to be, and
compared it to the realities of conscious living:*

I awake from my sleep, but I am held in a dream
My senses are on hold, yet split between
A link to this world and beyond
I nurture these thoughts and how to respond

Uniquely bridging both parts of my mind
I start to ponder what I might find
If in this moment, I were to die
In which of these worlds would I lie

Awake or dreaming, what would it be?
Death in reality, or in fantasy
No-one has been able to look inside
Life's great mystery, is classified

The Recession

The recession is with us, as if we didn't know
Our spending and spending has had to slow
Just the essentials, cutting back here and there
Should hopefully get us through this financial scare

But is this recession just one big scam?
That only affects the average working man
Politicians, lawyers and every big wig
Don't appear to be affected by this thingamajig

When your kitty is bulging, you can afford the best
Its mugs like us that are put to the test
The banks for instance have been hit quite hard
Ho what a shame, they played the wrong card

Are they told to put it right?
Not a chance, but the public funds might
That's our money they just use at will
Emptying our pockets for theirs to fill

Come on leaders get a grip
You've been complacent and let things slip
We put you in power and gave you our trust
Then we find...... 'Your heads are full of sawdust'

Capital Punishment

Let's reintroduce Capital Punishment
For years and years, it's been redundant
But since its exclusion from our laws
Violent crimes have soared and soared

An alarming coincidence it has to be said
But that's no consolation, to those who are dead
Violent crimes have increased without slowing
Do we really not know, why it's growing and growing?

The soft approach has certainly not inspired
The community we wanted and so desired
No public morals or sense if guilt
The lazy, the corrupt, we support to the hilt

Yet victims are abandoned, in this dangerous land
Slowly sinking in this crime quicksand
People need help and immediate support
Not false hope, in a massaged crime report

The prisons are full, bursting at the seams
Should we build more? In your dreams
Let's have a policy that clearly states
The gallows awaits.... those 'vicious mistakes'

Silence In Court

*I always wondered why the law of the land, allowed an accused person
the right to remain silent. Surely an innocent person could explain
where he was, or what he was doing? The prosecution should always
have to prove its case beyond reasonable doubt, but the scales of justice
should not be biased. Surely the game should be played on an even field.
Not with one opponent blindfolded and a hand tied behind his back!*

Every man has the right to speak in his defence
But not the right to hide behind silence
Law makers, it surely must be
The time to expose them for all to see

Let the truth of the facts decide what's right
Give law and order the chance to fight
Law makers, take notice of our demands
Lose the bias and free both hands

Now is the time to move things on
And side with justice, which seems to have gone
Law makers, open your eyes
Do not allow this silence of lies

Court room battles are won and lost
By lawyers playing games, at our cost
Law makers, this farce, has had its day
Those who commit crime, have to pay

Let's get back to a real deterrent
By ousting the law that's been inherent
Law makers, those guilty of crime
Should be sentenced to prison and do their time

Our lives seem so cheap, in this modern day
Why is it so easily taken away?
Law makers, our lives are very precious
We need your strength and wisdom…to protect us

No News Is Good News

Ok, Ok, we know money's tight
The economy dives deeper, every single night
Television, radio and newspapers too
Keep on reminding us, how everything's so blue

Let's have some good news, there's plenty to cheer
And shake off the depression, that's crept in here
Give us some respite from the moan and groan
If you hadn't told us, we wouldn't have known

Journalists record what's wrong and right
But I get the feeling it gives them delight
To keep on reporting depressing views
Sometimes! .... No news is good news

A State Of Affairs

Ho, what a state of affairs we are in
With politicians, getting under our skin
Sleazy, slimy, the pictures not good
Deep in the forest, lost in the wood

'Robin Hood,' stood for right above wrong
Where do these morals now belong?
Robbing the poor and the rich we see
Hooded and hidden by statute and complicity

No modern day hero for us to see
Who could we place into this category?
Political heads and government bodies
Look us in the eye and say, "no worries"

It's a world recession when things go bad
It's not their fault the economy is sad
When things are good and looking right
They take the credit with all their might

It's taken a while to see through this scam
They are drowning in blunder with no visible plan
How fickle do they think we are?
At the next election...... let's say, ta' ra'

My Legacy

Tonight I pondered a long deep thought
About my life and what it had brought
As a child growing up in the home
Then as an adult and how I have grown

I smile at life and all my dreams
And try to make sense of what it all means
My direction in life has meaning to me
I am where I am, and want to be

Memories fade into a distant past
Did you honestly expect them to last?
Then everything is lost, gone forever
Your existence wiped out, altogether

Was I good, or was I bad?
How irrelevant, isn't that sad?
All my efforts will soon disappear
Nothing remembered, in this biosphere

Just a few people will have made their mark
Leaving a footprint, so visible and stark
I leave you my poems, as my legacy to save
Will they be read beyond the grave?

Liquid Gold

The price of fuel makes it a liquid gold
So dam rare, at the price it's sold
Perpetual increases, they drive me insane
Forecourt costs have risen again

My car needs diesel it's my living, my job
But the government doesn't care, it continues to rob
By emptying my pockets when I pay out the cash
Before very long it will be ten quid a dash.

Taxed to the hilt, with cigs and beer
Fuel prices rise, year after year
The economy is crashing, it's on the skids
What a bleak future, for us and the kids

Who knows how far it will all descend?
Who will save us from this end?
Politicians! .... I don't think so
Not by the way I've seen things go

Lining their pockets without any shame
They pull the purse strings, in this economic game
Apologies and promises we have heard everyone
When will someone, finally get things done?

American Pie

How quickly four years has passed us by
Was it yesterday, we heard a nation cheer…then cry?
The most powerful man in the world was elected
His promise for tomorrow, got him invested

But our hopes and dreams, soon got dashed
When we went to war, then the stock markets crashed
Now a new leader, has come along
Banging his drum and singing the same old song

He will fight for justice, he walks a new path
He has seen the light, survived the aftermath
We believe the hype, we want it so much
It feels so close, it's almost…within touch

When his Office has duly been taken
Will many of the promises be forsaken?
Not forgotten, just put on hold!
Whilst the mess inherited starts to unfold

Will things really change? Will his broom sweep clean?
Will Barak Obama, fulfil the dream?
The world looks on with a smile and a frown
This is your destiny, don't let us down

The Olympic Game's 2008

Beijing opens China's gate
The world looks on to celebrate
The Olympic torch has found its way
Symbolically burning for the games to play

Athletes have gathered, united this day
Champions competing in a sporting display
Everyone has trained for four years or more
To win a medal and hear the crowd roar

Politics still tries to interfere
Raising new issues, year after year
All the cheap tricks and dirt they can throw
Won't stop the games or steal the show

Some individuals rise above the rest
Muscles are strained, fitness put to the test
Outstanding achievements can be won or lost
Pushing their bodies, whatever the cost

As the games draw to an end
We think to the next, where we hope to contend
Hard work and punishing routines
Face our Olympians in this theatre of dreams

Conflict

*When as a race will we ever be at peace with one-
another? How many thousands of years will have to pass
before we realise the futility of it all. Constant treaties are
made then breached. Fine words are spoken with good
intent, then little or nothing changes to eradicate this
continuing war.*

These troubles have raged since time began
Israel and Palestine will fight to the last man
How can they resolve this hereditary plight?
Can they agree, to put things right?

The world looks on and shakes it head
So many innocents make up the dead
How frustrating, to sit and listen
To so much stubbiness and so little wisdom

Each side is right, the other is wrong
I am tired of listening to the same old song
They are not alone in conflict and pain
The rest of the world shares this shame

Anger steeped in history, keeps rolling on
Until one or the other has finally won
But even then it won't stop this trial
There are no winners in war, it's brutal and vile

Africa

Africa, the land of dreams
But all we hear are cries and screams
Why the pain? Why so much sorrow?
All they want, is a brighter tomorrow

These people strive for a better life
Not hunger, hardship and so much strife
When will it change? I don't know
Will evil fall and goodness grow?

Their history shows no respite from gloom
Can they be delivered from this doom?
We can help to change their plight
By standing together and supporting what's right

Those that maim, kill and beat
Must never be allowed a parliamentary seat
They must be removed and made to pay
By delivering too them…their judgement day

The killing Fields

When children are used as human shields
In war zones, identified as killing fields
The reason behind it, you don't have to guess
Human pawns ...in a game of chess

Words cannot describe the anguish I feel
As news of the atrocities, is reported to reveal
Innocent children, torn Limb from Limb
To further the cause of some fanatical whim

Prohibited from attempting to stop this horror
We bow our heads and pray for tomorrow
Israel and Palestine, a conflict jamboree
Mankind in its lunacy, too blind to see

Hidden behind culture, religion and hatred
This kind of action, should not be tolerated
History has taught us over the years
That war brings nothing, but bitterness and tears

The Time Machine

My young son is a constant source of inspiration to me. He had to complete a school project titled the time machine. Whilst thinking about the probabilities of such a devise, I began to ponder these thoughts:

What laws of physics would we have to observe
To enable time travel, without life being disturbed
To visit the future and the past with hindsight
Avoid our mistakes, maybe put things right?

Time travel in the future is a probability
Making today's mistakes, a reversible possibility
This time window may cause us to inflict
More problems than solved, in any past or future conflict

Could we see wrong done and not put it right?
Just stand by, without a fight?
Just imagine the damage and possible devastation
Invoked, by tampering with natures creation

The most frightening thought, I hold in my mind?
Has the present been tampered with, by a future mankind?
What came before this? Were we saved from a hell?
Was it done for the better, only time will tell?

Life

*The sheer enormity of the universe and all its glory is
enough to blow your mind. So when you stop and
think about it, it's hard to comprehend what it's all
about? What does it all mean? Why did we evolve in
this way? Maybe one day when the universe has been
explored to its furthest point, we may come up with an
answer. Until then we can only guess and assume.*

Ponder this thought if you can
What was there, before life began
How did it start, when did it begin
What is this life force that burns within?

When we die, does it move on and go
Is it a force in perpetual flow?
Is this the difference between us and stone?
In a universe so big, are we really alone

In a world without life, there is no right or wrong
Nothing would matter, if it did, or did not, belong
But once life has started there are choices to make
They affect our survival, make no mistake

If life is so precious and the force carries on
Why do we age and then be gone
Is it a defect, or nature's way?
Of controlling our gift and having her say

Writers Block

There comes a time when your ideas and inspiration
suddenly dry up. I had a spell where the ideas were flowing
so fast I couldn't write them down quickly enough. Then I
got writers block and had a few weeks where I felt nothing
could inspire me again:

When the ideas in your head are just not there
You grind to a halt with a vacant stare
There are no ideas to get me flowing
No thoughts about anything, nothing growing

I wait for inspiration, knowing it will return
Writers block is the technical term
The mental juices will soon start flowing
But when will it happen? It's a worry, not knowing

I search for the key to unlock this dilemma
Sending positive thoughts to my creative antenna
Come on life, give me a clue!
Don't keep me waiting for the next big issue

Dyslexic Guy

My friend the dyslexic guy
Perceives things differently from his mind's eye
Messages and thoughts that leave his head
Appear rearranged and get misread

It's as confusing for him, as it is for you
When letters and figures appear untrue
He knows 4 plus 4 equates as 8
But this information is hard to translate

School said he was lazy and didn't try
Those were the hard times, in days gone by
Doctors now understand these symptoms much more
Diagnosed and treated they continue to explore

The avenues of the mind, so intricate and new
The symptoms of Dyslexia are no longer taboo
This invisible curse once lay undetected
Now we know, millions are affected

Call Of The Devil

Have you ever been driven to distraction or utter
despair by the actions of someone pressing the
self destruct button? How hard it is to stand by
and see someone you love destroy themselves. Yet
they seem oblivious to what they are doing and no
matter what help or assistance you give them, they
ignore it. These feelings of despair are echoed in
this poem...

She is consumed; surrounded by pain
Doing everything wrong, she cannot refrain
From the call of the Devil, she will gladly flock
To receive what he offers without taking stock

How hurt we have been at her slow demise
As she slips lower and lower, in front of our eyes
She is a beautiful girl, so tall and slim
But lacking that confidence and esteem within

She self abuses as her days slip by
So horrible a life, it makes me cry
But life goes on and there are choices to make
It's a slow process of healing that mends the break

Then a light shines through, and dents the fog
Can she reach out and grasp, a life saving log
As she flows down stream to a watery end
Which turn will she take? Her life will depend.

Poison Ivy

Tell a mistruth and let it be heard
Keep repeating it, however absurd
Then people will begin to think it's true
No matter how hurtful it is to you

Tell a mistruth, again and again
Those that tell them cannot refrain
The gossip that feeds and keeps them full
Makes them dislikeable and ever so dull

Tell a mistruth, it's a mischievous game
No credibility or substance and certainly no shame
They hunt and they forage trying to destroy
Reputations so fragile, as if playing with a toy

Tell a mistruth and target those who are nice
No skeletons in the cupboard to merchandise
The pot keeps calling the kettle black
One day these lies will pay them back

Tell a mistruth, there is jealousy and envy
For those that can't help themselves, get some therapy
Sort yourself out and leave others alone
Stop the bitching and please don't moan

Tell a mistruth and they prove what they are
Miserable, deceitful and such a liar
If you have nothing good, to do, or say
Keep your mouth shut, and your thoughts at bay

The Ride Of Your Life

How many heart beats has this symphony to play?
How long, until judgement day?
When life as we know it, will cease to exist
And we return to the bottom of our creators list

We are only mortals at the end of the day
We take what life throws at us come what may
Whatever happens, will happen you know
When the music stops, you have to go

The script is written, with a laid out plot
Received at birth and that's your lot
Sometimes it's hard for us to see
The routes mapped out, from A to Z

Destination unknown..... Enjoy the ride?
Maybe I'll see you on the other side
Who knows where or when it will be?
It's the ride of your life, just wait and see

Name Of The Game

Children should be nurtured as they grow and play
To develop their minds in society today
But in a world where violence, greed and hate
Are dished up daily, from the media plate

Unsupervised access, risks them crossing the line
They can lose sight of reality, in a world so sublime
A time bomb in the making, with a slow burning fuse
Our children in this environment have everything to lose

Then it happens, reported out of the blue
A story emerges, established as true
No fairytale or nursery rhyme
Babies making baby's before their time

How can we prevent these insane acts?
So that past statistics, don't become present day facts
Don't point the finger or lay the blame
Parents are responsible. It's the name of the game

Taxi Driver

I became a taxi driver because it allowed me to be my own boss and work flexible hours to fit in with my son's care. I have met many characters throughout the years and taxi drivers are unique. They get hassle from everyone, yet somehow they raise a smile in the face of adversity. If you are a taxi driver, you'll know what I mean. If you're not, take time to think about your behaviour and what we put up with, the next time you book a taxi...Drunk.

I became a taxi driver to earn some extra cash
My finances needed reviewing, they were under the cosh
I developed new skills for this hell of a job
As I drive Jeckle the nice guy and Hyde the yob

Why do punters think that once in my car?
The going rate's two quid, no matter how far
Can I smoke, can I drink, this pizza wont stain
You're a bad guy, a sad guy, if you try and refrain

How glad we all are when you decide to get out
Don't stand there talking and lounging about
Pay up and get going, you need to be quick
Its twenty five quid if anyone's sick

Don't slam my door, push your knees in my back
Put your hands on my windows and talk all that crap
Enjoy the trip, although I seem to speed
There are jobs in the office, from which I need to feed

Now some are ok and a pleasure to drive
They respect you as a person, have manners and behave
The job that I do has many facets within
I love it and hate it, but one day...I will pack it in.

Cafe Istanbul

*I had the pleasure of falling across a great little restaurant a few
Christmas' ago whilst out shopping. I thought the premises were a
cafe and went in for a sit down and a coffee. I was politely
informed of my mistake, but given coffee on the house whilst I
rested my laurels. I managed to secure a restaurant booking for
that same night as a cancelation was telephoned through. I have
enjoyed many meals in this restaurant which is situated in the
heart of Manchester City Centre. They never fail to serve what I
believe is the best Turkish food in town.*

The Cafe Istanbul, is a glorious place
A dining experience, you have to taste
Divine food, for you to consume
Inhale the East, as you enter the room

The ambiance; the perfect mood
Classically prepared, delicious food
The chef and staff all work as one
To seduce your hunger, it's so much fun

The finest of all Turkish cuisine
Plated out; a wonderful scene
First cruise the starters, it's hard to choose
Your heads in a spin and it's not the booze

Having chosen a starter, one, two or three
It's easy to spoil the main delicacy
Don't let your eyes rule your head
Or your stomach will ache as you are over fed

With perfect timing, grace and style
The waitress attends you with a smile
Wine and food perfectly flow
With a delicate balance of come and go

Suicide

*I was driving two men home in my taxi one night and
couldn't help overhearing their conversation about a friend
of theirs who had committed suicide. The man had recently
split from his wife and was going through an unwanted
divorce. He had custody of his teenage son who was also
going through difficult times. This domestic upheaval had led
to many arguments between father and son. One such
argument ended in blows. Full of remorse about striking out
at his son, and distraught over his marriage split, the father
had walked out of the house and committed suicide. The
story moved me so much that I wrote this poem after I had
dropped them off.*

Suicide, the key to an early grave
Those that do it don't want to be saved

A mind confused in utter despair
Could we have saved them? Do we care?

What a waste of a precious life
Too much hassle, too much strife

Too much pain, all built up within
Everything and everyone under your skin

I feel so trapped. No- where to go
My heads on fire it's going to blow

I cry out loud, although I don't speak
My will power to live, is dangerously weak

Maybe, when I am dead and gone
I can be at peace with everyone?

Reality Check

You wake up in the morning, too just another day
Everything seems sorted......then life goes astray
When news arrives of a sensitive kind!
The sort of stuff that blows your mind

Just when you think the spiral can't dip
Complacency sets in, allowing your guard to slip
Each day has a voice with something to say
And tomorrow brings...... whatever it may

So, whenever you feel on top of your game
Remind yourself...... now and again
Everything can be lost in the blink of an eye
This reality check...... will see you get by

Mobile Phone

The mobile phone is a wonderful device
But is it a devil, in disguise?
Always with us, no hiding place
Always obtainable and easy to trace

Let's debate the good and the bad
Examine the options, decide which to have?
The case against them is easy to see
Freedom and release from gadgetry

Not being controlled by a silicon chip
Protecting privacy not letting it slip
No more ring tones, to fry our brains
No more dyslexic, texting strains

How did we manage all those years ago?
People today don't really know
In a world so small and all alone
Without the assistance of the mobile phone

What do the pro group have to say?
They want this technology night and day
Always on hand to receive that call
The phone enables them to be in control

Mobile phones are the ultimate device
A dynamic tool at such a low price
Camera, recorder and game player to
The ultimate accessory for me and you

With the mobile phone, you can go anywhere
It's trendy, flash and great hardware
In the beginning, the size of a brick
Now so slim and elegantly slick

No matter what you think or say
The path of progress leads this way
Whatever the argument on this may be
The individual will choose. It's his right you see

Memories

*I was reminiscing about how it used to be; 'in the old day's'; when I
was a child. This was greeted with disbelief by my young son who
couldn't even imagine a world without his creature comforts. How the
standard of living has improved over the years. This gave me the
inspiration to write this poem and recall those memories:*

Winters here, my bones tell me so
Summers gone, the weather lets me know
When I was young, many years ago
I remember how cold and the falling snow

I remember the windows dressed with ice
Icicles on the inside, freezing, but nice
No central heating, just a coal burning fire
Projecting a picture from my minds desire

Foggy days, we called them 'Pea Soupers'
Wrapped up in duffle coats, scarves and jumpers
Clogs on our feet made from wood and leather
I wore them continually, whatever the weather

Our bath hangs on the outside wall
Brought in on Friday, to wash us all
Placed in front of a black-mantled hearth
My mother would wash us, eldest first

Oilcloth adorns the bedroom floor
Carpets were a luxury, but not any more
Coats on top, form a bedding quilt
So Jack Frost' hands could not be felt

I remember the summers always hot
Bursting road tar bubbles, pop, pop, pop
Those holidays in Wales by the sea
Two weeks every year, for our family

Sundays were special and we had a routine
Visiting the relatives that we hadn't seen
For tea, cake and a little talk
No car needed then, we were all within walk

Mystery Guest

Over the last few years I have enjoyed cruising holidays.
On one particular cruise, I was seated at a dining table
where a guest had not turned up. Every evening we
would look forward to the missing guest's appearance
but alas, they never came. The conversation would touch
on who they might be, or where they had come from? We
would try and visualise what they might look like and
what had caused their absence. Hence was born the
mystery guest.

We are dining aboard the Crown Princess
A floating experience, nothing less
The table is laid, guests expected
Then we realise, one's defected

The mystery guest, whoever they may be
Has evaded the pleasure of our company
Each night we await and try to guess
The unknown identity of our mystery guest

Illusive passenger where are you from?
You have forsaken our company, conversation and fun
So we toast this person every night
Raise our glasses and ponder what might

So will it be 'bon voyage' or 'bon appetite'
Mystery guest, turn up and eat
So unlike the fateful 'Marie Celeste'
We are only missing just one of our guests.

The Alabaster Shop

If you ever holiday in Egypt, it's quite probable that you'll
visit the Alabaster shop run by the crazy brothers three. Their
unique style of selling is an eye opener. The sales pitch is
vigorous, but tempered with humour and courtesy. You need
skin as thick as Rhino hide and a will of steel to secure the
best price. With the help of our guide we survived the
experience and bought 'Colin'.

Colin the camel has travelled a long way
A present for Sally from the holiday
Bought from Egypt as a bargain you see
From the Alabaster shop, run by the crazy brothers three

As we enter the room the theatre began
With the lights down low the 'Moon Stone' shone
Colin glowed bright, from the shelf at the back
So I leaned forward and lifted him off the rack

Prices start doubled, then are slashed to less
Your Egyptian pound will be put to the test
"Don't buy one sir, put three in your bag
Forget the price written on the tag"

You're expected to haggle before a price is agreed
"I give you a bargain sir; though I have a large family to feed"
So that's how Colin arrived back from over-sea
And now he glows for his new family

Wetting The Baby's Head

We all remember the joys of becoming a dad, whether it's for the first time or not. Isn't it wonderful how women put all the effort into child birth, then the men go out and celebrate it?

It wasn't me, so it must have been John, who casually let it be said
"It's time to honour the custom, of wetting the baby's head"

A serious drink was on the cards......and top of our agenda
So Thursday night was set aside, to have a serious bender

We drank our fill all through the night, until we couldn't drink no more
There was John, Barry, Dennis and Paul...... and Lee the brother-in-law

Conversations were slurred at the end of the night...... impossible to decipher
With vision blurred and senses gone my walking was even harder

As evening closed a glass was raised, to toast the little nipper
"Good health and happiness to the lad and mercy to the babysitter"

'Ahoy There'

*Apart from the many wonderful and interesting
places you visit when cruising, you also meet some
wonderful people and characters. During one of
these cruises we teamed up with a group of people
who were completely barking. None of us were
from the same background but the chemistry was
just right. Ian was so laid back he could have
fallen over. His wife Lil owned a flower shop and
was a hard working, self made woman. Rod was
retired and a handy man that enjoyed making and
selling good quality rabbit hutches. His wife Val
was a lovely woman who was interested in fish and
kept an aquarium. My alter ego on board ship ma-
terialised as Bronco Billy the karaoke man whilst
my side kick Jan has to be the coolest ship mate
that ever sailed the ocean.*

Rod, Val, Ian and Lil
Have all come aboard and met Jan and Phil
Rod 'the hutch' makes houses for his warren
Val 'the fish' gets tanked up about her aquarium

Ian 'the lad' is short, stout, dry and witty
Lil is 'potty' a florist in the city
Jan is a 'cow girl', smart lean and cool
Don't up-set her, she's no-bodies fool

Phil's a cowboy. 'Bronco Billy's the name.
Knife throwing and Karaoke are his game
Six 'sea dogs' all different, yet the same
None of them teenagers, but all insane

Troubled Waters

*My Halloween party was an open house as usual. A good mix
of family and friends made for a good night. Then one of my
mates got seriously drunk. Anyway without boring you with
the facts and before too much damage was done, he finally
came to rest in a drunken stupor on my bathroom floor. He
happily spent the rest of the night soundly asleep in the
bathroom. Appearing with a sore head and excuses the next
morning, his apologies were accepted, of course.*

My friend is such a lovely lad
But after a drink his behaviour's bad
He is a party joker and a pain in the arse
A dealer, a player, and simply quite crass

Everyone loves him and his cheeky smile
But beneath the mask, is he really that vile
He circles around from couple too couple
Humiliating and taunting, there is going to be trouble

At last extinguished is the spark of his flame
Collapsing and sleeping, he puts to bed the vain
When night lifts its veil and the day shines through
Revealed once again is the man so true

The demon within him has taken flight
And gone are the horrors of the night
Awake and sober he begins to think
What a 'Tosser' he is, under the influence of drink.

The Cue Master

*In the mid 1990's a very good work colleague of mine
called Phil McEwen, stuck a label on my snooker case
depicting that I was the cue master. He awarded me this
title because I caused the maximum amount of disruption
with the minimum of effort, either through total
incompetence, or just to make a person feel bad, were
his words. Even though I lost more than I won, the cue
master tag stuck. I wrote this poem after a good spell of
wins, just to wind my sons up. The label is still
cherished. Thanks Phil.*

Beautifully crafted was his two piece cue
Specially bought and boxed from view
Only taken out for the Master to play
Devouring opponents that stood in his way

No angle too difficult, his action so smooth
The cue master was awesome he knew every move
Snookers were flouted using cushions one, two and three
Make a mistake and he'll have an eight ball spree

Have a look, have a walk, and have a chalk
Quiet gentlemen please, no chatter, no talk
Practice every day and be at one with your cue
Then one day, my title may be bestowed on you.

The Tree

Tall and elegant, I look down from above
I open my arms to give life a hug
From this vantage point, I survey all around
But my feet are planted, firmly in the ground

Ringing the years as I slowly grow
I have weathered the seasons as they come and go
I stand alone, strong and proud
Harvesting life beneath my shroud

But you're killing me off with your constant abuse
Although I breathe life for you and all to use
So cut me down! Lay the land bare!
You'll join me in extinction when there's nothing there

Cigarettes

*If you are a non smoker, I think the next poem will
strike a few chords. If you are a smoker, try and
imagine the non smoker's point of view. Like anything
going on in a relationship both parties have to compromise. I wrote this poem after experiencing these
frustration…*

Smoke, smoke, it's everywhere
It's on your clothes and in your hair

It drives me crazy the smell is so vile
Just leave them alone, at least for a while

First thing in the morning, last thing at night
I just can't settle; is there no respite

I smell it on your fingers even where you're sat
It drives me crazy, I can't used to that

You are my perfect woman, in every other way
But your cigarettes are my dismay

The Secret Den

*One summer's day I took the kids out to my local
park and trekked around the undergrowth in a nature
quest. We fell upon a covering which we made into a
den. The kids played there all day, making it their
special home in the bushes and imaginations were
ignited.*

The weather was fine, it was a lovely day
So I took the kids out, they needed to play
The park was chosen it's an adventure playground
And whilst exploring, a secret den was found

It was hidden from sight, completely out of view
Inside a covering, big enough for two
The trees branched around and formed a hide
And we made an entrance from either side

A disused pallet and a plastic chair
Made it comfortable and homely inside the lair
A flag was made using a broken sign
Imaginations ignited, what a fabulous time

Additional branches helped us disguise
Any chance of discovery from prying eyes
The day passed slowly it needed to last
Proving simple things can give you a blast

No need for money or expensive toys
Just pure honest fun for me and the boys
Hidden away for another day
Our secret den was closed away

The Public House

The famous British pub is steeped in history and tradition. The strict licensing laws were changed recently to enable publicans to apply for their opening times to be changed. Many organisations feared that this change would create havoc. Has time proved them right or wrong?

The public house and licensee
A famous heritage steeped in history
Ancient customs and bar room wit
Have mirrored our society, into which we fit

Like a home we visit to socialise and play
For some it's a refuge, to hide away
Spirits, beer, soft drinks and wine
All served through the hours of opening time

The British pub, what an institution
Has poured itself into our constitution
Traditional, whacky, themed or real ale
The choice is endless, in this liquid sale

Whatever you fancy, it's all on hand
Drinking in pubs, will never be banned
They tried prohibition, in the United States
But soon repented, on their mistakes

Twenty four hours is the way we have gone
Some don't agree, but this right was won
Drink can flow from morning till night
But time will tell us, if we got it right

Airport Terminal

Anyone who's visited an airport terminal must have stood and
wondered in disbelief at the size of some of the queue's we endure. Is
there a better way to organise us and make our flying experience a
better one? The next few poems explore these thoughts:

D esigned for comfort, speed and ease!!!
The airport terminal, should be a breeze
But those who built it, forgot one thing
Our human comforts and understanding

The treatment of passengers is quite deplorable
It all boils down to what's affordable
Your welcome visit, is an open lounge
Standing in queues, for destinations bound

Queue's form quickly, then snake and weave
Your first experience is hard to believe
The foyer is busy, understandably so
But no thought was given to how it should flow

The check-in experience is such an ordeal
Can anyone believe, this is for real
Some move quickly and others slow
Whose fault is it? We will never know

Finally checked in, the bags disappear
Will we see them again? ....maybe next year!
The baggage workers wrestle the bags
Like prison wardens fighting the lags

Security checks by the dozen
But we don't mind, it's better than heaven
Passengers.....please don't despair
It's the price we pay to travel by air

Ship In A Bottle

*As a young boy growing up in the 1950's, I had to entertain
myself with hobbies and creative play. Television in those
days was in its infancy and children's programmes, although
available, were not broadcast in the variety they are today.*

*I remember making things out of elastic, wood, cardboard, or
anything I could scrounge or afford to buy. My thirst for such
a desire came from my father, who had a fascination for
finding out how things worked. He was very good at taking
things apart, but not as skilled at putting them back together.*

*From papier-mâché' puppets to model making we got
involved in doing almost everything. I recall with great
affection, the time my father and I made a ship in a bottle for
the very first time. This came in handy when my eight year
old son asked, "How does a ship get inside a bottle, dad?"
Explanations seemed complex, so I thought the best way to
explain it, would be to make one:*

The question was asked by my little lad
"How does a ship get in a bottle dad?"
I started to explain and noticed him frown
So I sketched out a plan and wrote it down

He liked the challenge, thought it would be fun
To have a go at making one
He found a bottle and I trimmed some wood
We mixed some plaster and things looked good

A touch of blue made the plaster a sea
And the wood made a boat glued together by me
We finished it off by plugging the gap
Not with a cork, but the original cap.

Christmas Spirit

The arrival of Christmas for many people brings with it a feeling of dread. The enormous pressure placed upon them to spend money at this time of year is immense. Why do we spend so much money? Is this what Christmas is now all about? Have we lost the plot? I was listening to an interview on the television where parents were explaining how much debt they had got themselves into just to cover the expense of Christmas. I felt sorry that people thought they had to celebrate it this way. Of course we like receiving and giving presents at this time of year, but we shouldn't be made to feel that this is the sole purpose of it.

Christmas has come and it's going to be fun
The presents are sorted; just the Turkey to be done

A festive holiday with too many chores
Hyped up, boozed up and full of bores

It arrives so quick and is gone so fast
Christmas that is, not the overdraught

Spend; spend; spend; regardless of the cost
The meaning of Christmas, totally lost

We seem to have forgotten what it's all about
It's not for presents, and buying shops out

It's a time for celebration, warmth and humour
To remember our Christ, born this time of year

A wonderful story about a man so good
Then the evil of man, drew his blood

So let's celebrate his wonderful life
Forgetting not, it was full of strife

Times then were hard, as they are today
So reflect on Christmas and what it has to say.

Today's Tomorrow

*This poem was written after a conversation with
three Irish lads. One agreed with me about being
positive and looking to the future, whilst the other
was wishing his life away and dwelling on past
regrets. The third just wanted to get through that day*

Look back and learn, don't dwell in regret
Today is tomorrow's, future outlet
Live for today, and forget what's gone
Yesterday has passed; tomorrow may never come

Don't worry about the past, or what might be
Now is the moment. Now is key
You can change the future, not what's gone
Be positive with your life and enjoy the run

Do not harbour, doubt, and sorrow
A positive attitude, brings a better tomorrow
Today is the beginning of the rest of your life
Change it for the better and eradicate the strife

Learn by your mistakes, don't blindly trundle on
Life is for living; embrace it; have fun
Life's not easy; we get knocks on the way
Paint the canvas and create today

Seize the moment, make it your own
You can do it. Only you alone
Get these thoughts, into your head
Remember these words; 'you're a long time dead'

The Road To Hell

Stuck in a traffic jam, it suddenly dawned on me how many cars were actually on our roads today. Who keeps buying them? Surely we must reach saturation point one day? How many more roads can we build before we run out of land?

The motorway, running from A to B
A concrete strip...... a vehicle community
Ploughing through the countryside, it twists and turns
A scar on the landscape, we have carved and churned

Millions of cars, burning rubber each day
Roads for motorists, here to stay
Two lanes, three lanes and now its four
But sooner or later they will build some more

Suddenly the traffic grinds to a halt
Stop rubber necking, of course it's your fault
Is it an accident, maybe a repair?
Everyone slowing in order to stare

Carry on with your journey, let's get home
Keep on moving, and get off your phone
Pumping fumes into the atmosphere
Destroying the world we love so dear

We can't continue to abuse it this way
We have to control it, keep it at bay
No living space, our future is doomed
Just one huge freeway, pumping fumes

Concrete and tarmac, will be our national treasure
Future generations, will know no better
So come on everyone, let's get green
Canvass your politicians, be heard and seen

The Twilight Man

The twilight man is the taxi driver who stays on when all the other drivers have gone home. He provides cover for the office and conveys people to the airport or takes the very late, or very early person home, or to work.

The twilight man drives from dusk to dawn
A lonely figure, with features drawn
His rest will come all too soon
When at close of shift he sleeps until noon

The office stays open to feed him what may
Revellers want home after a very long play
The roads are quiet; peace and calm ensue
Occasionally broken by the boys in blue

King of the road at this unearthly hour
His passenger's are quiet and feeling dower
Night finally awakes and cracks a smile
Natures deciding; will she be nice or vile

The Phoenix Four

Would you believe it, it's happened again
Money squandered, on a gravy train
Forty million pounds just frittered away
Plus sixteen million, 'to review it', they say

In trying to help the workforce out
Greedy directors were allowed to flout
The laws and rules that govern their behaviour
Lining their pockets at the expense of labour

The government has tried to keep afloat
A leaking vessel, a dodgy boat
With lots of money for its restoration
They had little or nothing to do in its floatation

Not controlling what was done or said
The company funds were simply bled
This appropriation...... is beyond a joke
As the tax payers money goes up in smoke

A corporate body again gets help
But when they abuse it, do we get a scalp?
Maybe the piper, should start playing his tune
Instead of sweeping mistakes with a political broom

The Phoenix four say they are not to blame
They should hang their heads, heavy in shame
Investing four pounds...... What did they get back?
Security and a future, for engineering the sack

The Wishing Well

Hey! ...... Our leaders have got this great idea?
On how to resolve, the poor Nation panacea
All the rich countries will create a fund
And let it be heard......orotund

Billions will be available, each and every year
In an act of kindness, we all can share
Every leader and head of state
Will have a say, in this global debate

But as the talk circles around
Good intentions disperse into the ground
They can't agree on the size of their share
Whatever is donated......has to be fair!!

They did agree that it was the right thing to do
And that the fund was real and not taboo
After days of argument, a common ground was struck
The money isn't available...... 'Although things are looking up'

Political leader's stop this debate
People are dying...... they can't wait
Words aren't enough, let's get things done
This is a motion that has to be won

Easy Come, Easy Go

Easy come, easy go
What's the cost, do you know?
Do kids appreciate what's been bought?
Teach them the lessons that need to be taught

Easy come, easy go
Things in life aren't free you know?
They have to be earned by you and me
Then received with gratitude and humility

Easy come, easy go
Save your money and watch it grow
Don't throw it away, it's easily spent
Then your bank account, show's a serious dent

Easy come, easy go
A fool and his money are soon parted you know
Everyone takes and they let you give
They will empty your pockets as fast as a sieve

Easy come, easy go
What's important, do you know?
It's not a crime to do without
So give it a try and leave it out

Demon Child

New relationships are exciting but can be very stressful, especially if one or the other has children from a previous relationship. This poem was written for a friend of mine, who was being driven crazy by the antics of his partner's son.

Demon child where are you from?
Are you really the devils son?
Some days good, some days bad
So much disruption from such a young lad

Demon child were you sent from hell?
Satan's son, has come to dwell
Wreaking havoc instead of good
Denying them peace, like he should

Demon child you are such a pain
I feel exhausted, it's blowing my brain
Every day I try to work you out
Every day I try not to shout

Demon child make our family one
I want to treat you like my son
How nice it would be, to laugh and smile
Then you could be.... my perfect child

The Apartment Block

*Noise can be one of the most irritating and frustrating
things to deal with. Love your neighbours or hate them, we
are sometimes stuck with them. Unfortunately for some, they
live next door to a noisy neighbour. This poem was written
in response to the frustrations felt by an inconsiderate and
very noisy neighbour.*

I live in an apartment on the second floor
The place is a palace, somewhere I adore

Positioned just right on a beautiful estate
Everything was perfect, but I'm getting irate

The neighbour above me, has a wooden floor
And I hear every movement, at every hour

Now wooden floors are definitely out
The tenancy agreement carries such clout

So please quieten down in your haven above
And give those below, some neighbourly love

Moments In Time

Life can be richer, when it is shared
With a person you love, perfectly paired
Moments in time that we nurture and defend
An existence with meaning, something to comprehend

Life with no structure, order, or routine
Is useless and effortless, a floating dream
A life without motive, is a life without means
A life that is wasted, seems totally obscene

Like a verse without lyric or a song without melody
A play with no stage, drama, or tragedy
No past, no future, or even a present
Just moments in time, without intent

This place is empty, a bottomless pit
A Romeo lost, without his Juliet
But having each other they continue to strive
In a world where their bond, will flourish and survive

The Hoody

*I was listening to the news one night and had to smile
at the irony of a young thug protesting his right to
wear a hood that covered his face from view. Human
rights and free speech are the foundation of our
society. There is a minority that abuse these rights in
order to hide their identity whilst committing crime. If
it wasn't so outrageous, it would be laughable.*

I'm a Hoody! I hide my face from sight
I don't want you to see me. Is that alright?

Having a good night out, later today
Getting pissed up, or doing a line, if I may?

If I kick someone's head in, it's a bonus to boot
But if that doesn't work, I might pull a gun out and
shoot

Don't worry, not face to face, or one to one
Because the odds aren't big enough and I risk getting
done

It's a laugh with my mates, kicking arse around town
Causing havoc, disruption and larking around

But the coppers keep bugging me, always on my case
Have they nothing better to do…they are a total
disgrace

Bubble Wrap

The driver shield was designed to protect the private
hire taxi driver from attack. You don't need
something like that, you might say. We wouldn't hurt
the person driving us home? Well let me assure you
there are a lot of people who do. Unfortunately
many taxi drivers are assaulted each year and some
are even murdered. What a job?

The bubble wrap shield is a guard against crimes
It provides protection in these dangerous times
The plastic shield does the job
Protecting drivers from the yob

The full wrap shield fits around your seat
Secured by the head rest and a belt so neat
Two months in and it stops any surprises
A great bit of kit, with no complicated devices

Passengers keep saying they haven't seen it before
So stop asking the question, it's beginning to bore
Keep your hands to yourself and off the screen
This helps not to mark it and keep it clean.

The Runner

A few people think that a free ride home is ok. Well it is, if the taxi driver allows it. The thing is, if they did that for everyone, they wouldn't earn any money would they? However, it still happens now and again and it's irritating to say the least.

They book a taxi with no intention of paying
Doing a runner, is the proper saying
They have no conscience, it's been done before
They are despicable people, we all deplore

We sometimes ask for the money up front
When out of town, you may do a bunk
Some get away with it, if no money is demanded
Being taken for a mug makes the crime so
compounded

They make their excuses to get out of the car
Some are plausible with a cheeky repertoire
They say "thanks for the ride," then they run
With no payment made, you lose another one

Good Night

How does one cope with the loss of a life
partner? The pain and emptiness seem so unfair
and difficult to come to terms with. Yet life
carries on for the other, who suddenly has to
cope alone.

L ife's long partner or so it seems
Say "good night," then no more dreams
Two cups, two saucers, two spoons, two hearts
Two souls together then one departs

Two people in unison, a compatible delight
Why have you left me, and taken flight?
Laid to rest, having passed away
No plans can be made for this saddest day

Good night my love, sweet dreams forever
One day again we will be together
I wait for the time when I am called to go
My creator has spoken......Oh please......not too
slow

Remember Me

*How times seem to have changed. Sometimes not for the
better when it concerns our old folk. It seems that in this
modern day and age, everyone is either too busy or
preoccupied to care about the elderly, unless their help is
needed. So just think about the elderly for a moment, as
one day you will hopefully become one. They have
contributed so much to make our society what it is today,
and we sometimes forget that, in life and after death.*

Growing old demands respect
We have given our love, effort and intellect

Do you care if I am happy, sad, indifferent or kind?
Does it really matter, does anyone mind?

We make ends meet as life slips by
Will anyone remember me, after I die?

To the few we remember, they are set quite apart
From all the people who had to depart

Soon forgotten and quick to dismiss
Why do our families treat us like this?

Marriage Lines

I wrote this poem for my son's wedding. It say's so
much about them and I was more than honoured to
read it out at the ceremony.

The story continues and can't be undone
They are lovers, buddies, all rolled into one
The bride and groom have come a long way
Since they fell in love, on that auspicious day

Two hearts, two minds, a couple in tune
So much love and devotion, no chance of doom
Survivors they are, having done better than most
Others have fallen, before the finishing post

Let's cast our minds back to 1992
To Labella's in Monton where love shone through
With Ste Denny the matchmaker, they had a few beers
Starting a life full of happiness, empty of tears

Cementing their love by marriage they show
Hard work and effort make a relationship grow
Peel Green's finest and the prodigal son
Are today joined in marriage, witnessed by everyone

The Operator

Sometimes moody, sometimes a grump
More often than not, she gets the hump
She sometimes panics, thinking her life's on hold
But deep within, beats a heart of gold

Working the office she juggles the jobs
Call taker and door person, she controls the yobs
Everyone loves her, drivers and clientele
Don't upset her she has a temper from hell

Keep your chin up girl and crack a smile
Keep the jobs rolling in; I like my lifestyle
No feeding. No favourites. You know the score
Your reputations intact; unlike others shown the door

So when your heads exploding and you're in a whirl
Just remember.... you're our favourite girl
From Parr socialite, too Sutton Dame
Who's that bossy operator! .... Nicky's her name

No Pick-Up

You are a person out for the night
Who books a taxi home
I am the consequence of your call
Made through your telephone

Patiently waiting I look out for the fare
Then, I start to recall
I ponder the fact, you have let me down
And the taxi, isn't needed at all

So pompous in drink and self esteem
No regard for what you do or say
Obnoxious minds turn and churn
As night dispenses day

Oh, you ignoramus.
The one that drinks from the medalling cup
You don't give a dam about me or the lads
It's just another ......' no pick-up'

Mr Nicotine

This is a guy who gets under your skin
If you're daft enough, to let him in
He'll poison your mind and drive you insane
With his constant demands, calling your name

He is 'addiction', with a friendly smile
Making you like him, but really quite vile
You can't get enough, he's eating you away?
You have to be strong or he's here to stay

Mr Nicotine, you are an evil man
Release my friend, if you can
People would leave you, if they could
You're more controlling than any class 'A' drug

Is this a marriage made in hell?
I don't know, only time will tell
"I am going to quit. Very soon"
Will be the epitaph on your tomb

The Fall

The sky kept its promise and delivered the call
Today was the day, it started to fall
Softly descending, then dusting the ground
Everything covered, so silent, no sound

Then the kids…with parents in toe
Slide and fall, wherever they go
This picture post card, sets the scene
A blanket of white, where it used to be green

The cold bites hard and unleashes it's wet
But the faster you run, the warmer you get
Laughing and screaming with every slide
Enjoyment for everyone who seem satisfied

Except the motorists and those not at play
Who curse and swear at this heavenly display
Disrupted services, people off work
February's the month, it all goes berserk

Spin

Who puts the spin on the news?
Who decides what to use?
Who decides what to keep or scratch?
Who's the person wielding the axe?

Where is the voice that's meant to be true?
All it does is try to mislead you
Is it a device, skilfully crafted?
For hype and hysteria, cleverly drafted

Look outside of the Potting shed
Not everything in life, is as it's said
Don't believe everything they feed
You know what they say about 'sowing the seed'

When facts are reported as truthfully portrayed
Sometimes they're not and conveniently purveyed
So watch which stories you decide to spin
Or you may end up...... with egg on your chin

The Dark Side

*The romantic poems in this section of the book
need no explanation as to their origin. Many of
these poems have been written from heartfelt
experiences, whilst others are pure fantasy.
Emotions fire the engine that burns inside each
and every one of us. I feel sure that you will
identify the many emotions that you yourself have
felt, past and present.*

She is poisoned by a friendly kind
Swept up in passions almost blind

He is the demon of tortuous beguile
An impotent symbol desperate to defile

Weaving through every contrived word
He breathes contempt, it's quite absurd

He is the master puppeteer
Pulling the strings of hearts so dear

The final act is yet to come
Who will his axe fall upon?

Dreams

Dreams require a dreamer
They have imagination and hope
Dreams are what life is made up of
Without them how can we cope?

Dreams can be a fantasy, lost within a sleep
Others are goals we strive to meet
To follow a dream we might like to aspire
A secret yearning a burning desire

Nothing is better than a dream come true
But if you don't make it try not to be blue
Let dreams be a release instead of a need
Unconscious impulses for our brains to feed

So whatever your dream, live life to the full
Be modest, content and never dull
Never stop dreaming it's a human trait
A god given blessing and not a mistake

Home Alone

Her mood had changed, now it was night
A sorrowful yearning was taking flight
She was hesitant to make the journey home
Without the drink, she was now all alone

Engulfed by feelings of utmost dread
Woeful thoughts crept into her head
Her eyes were full and just a cry away
Alone this Christmas, no festive day

How can I awake to my first Christmas alone?
In an empty house, now an empty home
Hard times exist for many and more
Like an open wound, it leaves you sore

The healing process in time will repair
These desperate feelings of utter despair
Rising from the ashes, a Phoenix re-born
You will rewrite the page, from which you are torn

Secret Admirer

You are the person I secretly admire
You are my fantasy, the one I desire
With thoughts locked away inside my head
I speak volumes to you, without a word being said

I caught sight of you the other day
Your head was turned in such a way
That the light caught your hair and threw off a shine
You looked serene, so very divine

You are beyond my reach and infinite touch
Yet you stir me inside, I want you so much
Your presence is powerful, the attraction so great
I ache to embraces you, but have to wait

Maybe that day will never come
Maybe as always, I turn and run
Oh what a coward, how spineless I am
In the passage of time you found another man

It doesn't matter that I love you so
Because these thoughts of mine, you will never know
When we meet and pass the time of day
I withhold this secret and keep my feelings at bay

Love And Marriage

This marriage was established, forty years to date
On April the first, nineteen sixty eight
Told by many that it would end in tears
This date proved significant over the years

Lovers, buddies, all rolled into one
Forsaken by family, they triumphed and won
Charlie and Margaret have come a long way
Since they fell in love, on that special day

Two hearts, two minds, a couple in tune
Such energy, such charisma, no chance of doom
Survivors they are, having done better than most
Others have fallen, before the finishing post

So let's look back to where it all began
Scotland's finest and the prodigal son
Vows were taken at Haymarket Reg
Where Margaret picked up.... her meat and two veg

Night Vision

*Most sea views are spectacular. However, late one night,
whilst stood on board ship sailing around the Caribbean,
I was relaxing and looking out over the vast expanses of
ocean. The moon was shining onto the sea through a
band of wispy clouds that highlighted the white wave
crests, as if a beam of light had been switched on. The
horizon could just be seen in the distance. The view was
heavenly and the moment magical.*

Cloaked by clouds, half hidden yet bright
The moon illuminates a corner of the night

Almost black with touches of white
Wave crests dance without respite

The clouds stretch out and open their hands
Stroking the sky in shimmering bands

A breath of wind so warm and soothing
Caressing, touching and gently moving

The horizon curves in a distant bow
Natures canvass delicately balanced somehow

Moulded by a creator so eloquently skilled
A masterpiece drawn, a masterpiece unveiled

The Awakening

The attraction was instantaneous, it was later said
Feelings welled inside her, followed by a flush of red

First meetings never do this! Surely feelings have to grow?
What was it about him that stirred her so?

He caught his breath! She was beautiful, in bloom
His gaze lingered, as their eyes met across the room

What was it about her? So extraordinary in every way
The awakening within him had been sleeping...... until this day

He smiled and introduced himself, then softly took her hand
She held the grip, just long enough, for him to understand

She looked in his eyes, soul searching for any trace
And found her dreams, written upon his face

The Odd Couple

Captain sensible and princess snuggle bum
Two people in love and having fun

He is crazy. As mad as a wasp
His actions and behaviour have everyone lost

But he means no harm with his jokes and teases
With these innocent gestures he hopefully pleases

She is a princess, so elegant and proud
But her shyness prevents her from being allowed

To flash all her assets, she has wrapped up and hidden
So the captain looks on, but is quite forbidden

Her charms are clearly the very best
Perfectly formed curves flutter under her vest

With long slim legs and a washboard tum
She is finished off with the perfect bum

Mother Of Mine

I found a poem, written by that mother of mine
On a piece of paper, suspended in time
Hidden away to be found one day
She describes her life in such an eloquent way

She wrote:

We met and married, a long time ago
  We worked long hours and the wages were low
No TV or wireless...... as times were hard
Just a cold water tap and a walk in the yard

No holidays abroad or carpets on the floor
There was coal on the fire and no lock on the door
Our children arrived, no pill in those days
We brought them up, without state aid

Children were safe going out in the park
Old folk too, could walk in the dark
No valium, no drugs, and no LSD
We cured much of our ills, with a good cup of tea

No vandals, no muggings, there was nothing to rob
We felt we were rich...... with a couple of bob
People were happier, in those far off days
Kinder and helpful, in so many ways

Milkmen and paper boys would whistle and sing
And a night at the pictures...... was our 'mad fling'
We all had our share of trouble and strife
We just had to face it. That was the pattern of life

Now I'm alone, I look back through the years
I don't think of the bad times, the trouble, or the tears
I remember the blessings, our home and love
And that we shared them together, I thank god up above.

Jean Royle (Deceased 15.7.02)
Not dated, but found on 24.3.09

Meltdown

So confused! Don't know what to do!
His head's in meltdown and he's feeling blue
Choices to make, but he cannot choose
Whatever he decides he's going to loose

He doesn't want to be cruel, just do his best
So exhausted......He needs some rest
It's not that easy...... to leave......just go!
The pressure's too great, his minds going to blow

Just a few days will see him through
Then he will know, what to do
All he needs......is get his head right
Get focused and see the light

When you're drowning and cutting no slack
Nothing in life is white, or black
So whatever decision you decide to take
Make sure it's not...... your biggest mistake

Strolling Along

It was a grey day, but the rain held off
It was windy, cold and the ground was rough
So we decided to drive and then we walked
Oblivious to everyone we strolled and talked

Hers arms were around me and I held her tight
Two spirits in unison; everything so right
Our destinies achieved in this perfection of days
Our journey had begun in so many ways

She is stunning and elegant and I love her so
This walk had to last, so the pace was slow
Old times were relived along this journey into the past
Exchanging stories we cuddled and laughed

How glad he was that his time was shared
With a woman so incredible no one else compared
Their walk was completed and at an end
But the future was theirs to share and spend

Their days no longer hit and miss
Two hearts, two minds, in total bliss
How strange life is, with its twists and turns
If you're prepared to wait, this can be earned

The Rings

United by love so beautifully defined
These two people are two of a kind
It grows and grows, day by day
So they decided to celebrate, in a special way

Not by ceremony or legal mumbo jumbo
But a powerful sign that will never bow
They decided on rings that would clearly show
Their hearts are each others, where no other can go

They wanted rings that were totally unique
Signifying a love so complete
Then, in St. Martin, they were seen
Produced by a jeweller, who fulfilled the dream

Magically conjured before their sight
Two matching rings in yellow and white
Expertly crafted in 18ct gold
The moment they saw them, they were sold

Her ring slipped on, a perfect fit
His needed altering......only a bit
Worn with pride for everyone to see
They were offered and accepted without complicity

Love

Can love be touched or is it pure inspiration?
Is it something we feel? Or is it something just spoken?
Is it something done during the course of a day?
To make someone feel special in a particular way

Should love be blind, or a compromise?
Is it that tingle you get, as you look in their eyes?
Does your heart skip a beat, in the middle of the day?
Does the mere thought of them, take your breath away?

Do they enter your dreams in the middle of the night?
Set your mind on fire...... knot your stomach so tight
Then love is a feeling, that sensation you feel
A feeling within, you cannot conceal

Does your heart constantly ache and your body go all coo?
Are you roused from your sleep...... with passions anew?
Yes...... I do
When I think of 'you'

Dream Lover

I was dreaming about you, again last night
We actually made up and put things right
Things were perfect between you and me
Together again, like it used to be

I tried so hard in those early days
To please you and woo you in so many ways
But sharing and caring has to be divided
It has to be equal and not all one sided

Now those days are all long gone
Time is slowly trundling on
But there still remains until this day
A part of me that you stole away

All our memories are kept stored inside
Some rise to the surface, but are now classified
Others remain hidden and don't reappear
You were my dream lover that is no longer here

Sea View

A splash of turquoise fringed with white
Colours the ocean as the waves take flight
As the curtain of water gathers as blue
Somewhere in the distance, the ocean's made new

The sky was clear as the sun shone through
But up ahead, it wasn't that true
A single cloud, scouting alone
Stretched back its reach, as if beckoning home

Others rallied with a jeer
Then water was shed, from the atmosphere
After dowsing the ship they passed on by
Returning the sun, to a clear blue sky

The horizon keeps promising a dream sunset
But the clouds keep mustering as if to protect
Our patience was rewarded on the very last day
When the sun rested its head, in such a beautiful way

Lovers In Love

Pure love has touched me, it strokes away my pain
You entered my life, I feel born again
Why has god from high up above
Blessed me, with this, your precious love

Your eyes sparkle, as you turn your head
It tells me everything and not a word is said
Your lips are soft and your kisses so, so sweet
I close my eyes and my dreams are complete

Teasing and touching we slide into bliss
How could we have known it would be like this?
Pandora's Box opened. Emotions fly wild
I hunger for love, I am such a child

Love craves an anger that cannot be understood
It cuts and it hurts, without drawing blood
Why do we allow it? Can it be explained?
Are we mental, stupid, or even deranged?

My heads in a spin, I feel sick and weak
There are no answers for what I seek
Will someone solve this eternal dilemma?
So that our love survives and we can be together

Gladys' Bar

Whilst sailing the Caribbean, we pull into port
The ship drops anchor as we prepare to cavort
Brightly coloured houses, dotted here and there
Protrude from the backdrop, in a vivid stare

Cast against the sky line, the view is divine
Picture perfect, everything in rhyme
The islands flirt, titillate and tease
Tree tops sway in a delicate breeze

Everyone different, but each a delight
A spectrum of colour, an amazing sight
Blue seas caress the coves of white sand
Conjuring thoughts of pirates and contraband

In St Thomas we visit Gladys' bar
A great little place, that's not very far
Just off the main road, through a few alleyways
One of the highlights, in so many ways

The food is good and the beers are cold
Their chilli sauce, Wow!! You've been told
Gladys the song bird, is always in tune
As warm as summer and always in bloom

She performs for everyone at no extra cost
Precious moments, never to be lost
These memories are personal and totally unique
A treasure locked away for me to keep

Deep Space

There is a place you take me
It's somewhere deep within
A strange unchartered territory
Where no-one else has ventured in

This deepness stirs and frightens me
I discovered it because of you
It's like an out of body experience
From which I look down and view

I am floating in emotions
Our souls touch as one
I languish in these feelings
Where have they come from?

They are deeper than Atlantis
Impossible to explain
Beyond the reach of normality
Housed in a distant domain

For some this place is unreachable
That seems so very unfair
This deep space is so incredible
One day, I hope you make it there

The Embrace

L ying beside you I feel an awesome thing
A warm embrace make's my heart sing
A melody of feelings all rolled into one
A feeling of contentment, second to none

With your head on my shoulder, we snuggle in tight
I feel your love, everything's so right
Your breath is gentle and caresses my ear
As our arms embrace, there's only love in here

No words are spoken. This silence needs no speak
I feel so strong, yet I feel so weak
Sleep beckons, as night closes in
I touch and I stroke, your beautiful skin

My face meets yours and then we kiss
So gentle and powerful.... utter bliss
Your hand strokes my body with a velvet touch
My minds on fire, I want you so much

Together we feel totally at one
Holding each other as sleep trundles on
Held so tight in a loving embrace
We drift into dreams with a smile on our face

The Post-It Note

It's a little game he likes to play
When she's gone out shopping, for the day
The house is quiet and he looks around
He sniffs out hiding places, like a bloodhound

Hand written messages are hidden to be found
Love notes, jokes and pictures abound
They have to be discovered on a journey through the night
When at each port of discovery they bring delight

It's silly, childish, juvenile fun
But to me it's a gesture, to my chosen one
It's nice to know someone's thinking of you
These notes of affection, prove it's true

So the next time you're sitting home alone
And the ringer hasn't rung on the telephone
Take a look and check it out
There might be a surprise lying about

A hidden note might be waiting for you
But there again it could be two
Two may become three or many more
So keep on looking and have an explore

Hair Of The Dog

*Having a drink with your mates is great fun. However,
now and again I seem to get a thirst on, and this is
when they seem to slip down quite easily.*

*Unfortunately, when you have one or two more than
usual there are consequences to bear. I awoke to one
such morning and wrote this poem...... after I'd taken
the tablets:*

I went out last night and had a drink or two
Woke up this morning feeling blue
That few little drinks I have now and again
Are usually ok, but now I'm in pain

I didn't really notice, as one became two
Then two became more than just a few
By the time I realised, it was far too late
Now I'm nursing a huge headache

It's my mates you know, I blame them completely
Encouraging me to drink so obscenely
If it wasn't for them and all that peer pressure
I wouldn't get plastered, I'd feel much fresher

I know my limit. I know when to stop
When the barmaid calls time and says "drink up cock"
That's when we leave, wave and blow kisses
Then home to bed without waking the missus

It costs me a lot, to get in this state
A night of bear swilling and oral debate
Then morning appears and my heads full of grog
But I know how to clear it? With the hair of the dog

Puppy Love

Month after month, but it feels like years!!
My son has constantly pounded my ears
He wants a dog, to love and look after
But this family addition, would be a disaster

There are periods in time, with no mention of the hound
When my guard is down, a new attack is found
With repeated vigour, he bombards me again
"Can I have a dog.......I've thought of a name"?

I begin to weaken, the pressure's too great
Advice is given, but it's far too late
I have started to plot, and even scheme
How to fulfil, the four legged dream

When my head clears, I suss things out
My role will be nurse-maid, to a very wet snout
Cleaning and feeding would be my domain
Whilst my son does walkies ....now and again!!

Peter The Rabbit

Peter the rabbit has come to stay
A new patio at home prompts his holiday

Staying with granddad for a week or two
Has saved him from becoming...... a rabbit stew

Quiet at first, then he went quite crazy
And set about digging in a garden frenzy

Holes here, holes there
My garden's a colander and I start to despair

That big crazy rabbit thinks he is staying
I see him plotting and even surveying

My gardens disappearing before my eyes
Is this a rabbit or a Mole in disguise?

Then the news, right out of the blue
He's not returning, he is staying with you!

The Great Escape

Peter the rabbit jumped the fence today
Tried to escape, run away
Pastures new, a place forbidden
A great escape, into another garden

My neighbour called round in such a panic
Peter was there and going manic
Jumping and prancing in sheer delight
Peter was unstoppable and dashed out of sight

The problem arose, can we get him back
So we teamed up together and formed an attack
I went this way, she went that
Hoping to spring our cunning trap

He saw our plan, what was on the agenda
So he vaulted back, rather than surrender.
Back where he belongs and his breaches fixed
He seems content, so no more tricks.

Sure Thing

A horse racing fanatic was having his say
When he mentioned a 'sure thing' for the very next day
He was pretty certain about a particular horse
That was running a race, at a certain course

A reliable source had given him the tip
A sure thing for certain, if it didn't trip
Have a flutter it's a cert for you
The meetings at Salisbury, at ten to two

I decided to have a little flutter
Risking a few pounds that didn't matter
Should I tell my mates and let them know?
Or keep it to myself in-case it runs slow

I pondered my options and went for a win
Wrote out the slip and handed it in
I passed it to the girl, my actions quite quick
Kissed my money goodbye and then felt quite sick

The smell of a win was being aired
Was it a premonition, or was I running scared?
The horse started fast then fell behind
A failure this time, but never mind

I staked my money and took a chance
Leaving pockets empty, in jacket and pants
The moral of the story has got to be
There are no winners in betting, except the bookie

It's Only A Game

The taxi rank can become a theatre, where
camaraderie, tricks and repartee are provided in
abundance. I was sat watching three of the lads kicking
a football about, during a quiet spell. The rest is
history:

I'm watching three men, kicking a ball
Playing footie and trying to recall
Those youthful days forever lost
Who can't get them back at any cost!

They pass it around like three little kids
But their fitness is waning, it's on the skids
They run themselves ragged, bellies hanging out
Panting and wheezing, kicking the ball about

Up in the air, lobbed, headed and saved
They have no control as the ball misbehaves
Curling this way, spinning that
They couldn't even hit...... the Watford Gap

Give it the boot and call it a day
Your memory deceives; you could never play
Come on lads, please take a break
I'm laughing so much, my sides ache.

Empty Head

I pick up every Tom, Dick and Harry
Driving around, in my job as a cabbie
In and out of the car each day
I am never surprised at what passengers say

Two women saw a pub sign clearly displaying
Parking at the back, live group playing
What a funny name for a group, said one
The other acknowledged her, with a tut and a hum

I tried to intervene and have my say
But they carried on regardless in their drunken way
Sarcastically I offered my point of view
They will never be as good, as that 'New Menu'

I naturally assumed this would get a good response
These two were competing, for the title of 'class dunce'
Never heard of them either...... the same one said
I blew out a sigh and thought...... 'Empty Head'

The Zoo

I like the wacky warehouse
It's down the road from where I live
I get to go ape in there
And play with all the kids

A caged in pandemonium
Provides the perfect kiddie club
There are slides, ropes and climbing frames
Conveniently inside the pub

My dad also likes it in there
So he can sit and have a think
But why does all this relaxation
Require so much drink?

Brewster calls into the pub
To surprise us whenever he can
The big brown bear is just the treat
But inside, it's just a man

We tease the bear and gather around
To try and pull his tail
But even though he twists and turns
We never seem to fail

Day after day, he thrills the kids
We couldn't ask for more
He deserves a medal, I hear them say
Even club bouncers have refused this door

Dad's Yommer

Everyone knows 'someone' who uses a knife as a screwdriver, or attempts to hammer screws into brick walls. Someone who attempts any home improvement project, although they are hopeless at it. Then there's the one special tool that is used for every D.I.Y venture, regardless of whether it's suitable for the job or not.

Dad's yommer was the nickname of such a tool. This legendary claw hammer, ruled supreme in my friend's home for as long as she can remember. She still has the hammer to this day, and loving recalls the antics surrounding its unorthodox use. These facts are true and have not been altered to protect the innocent!

'Dad's Yommer,' is a legendary tool
A stubby claw hammer, red taped, and cool
It knocks in screws and chisels brick
In fact; "There's nowt that can't be done with it"

No job too big......no job too small
The Yommer is used to do them all
When the carpet in the lounge started to creep back
He screwed it down, with a six inch tack

No need for a drill, or suitable bit
Dad took aim and then...... Just hit it!
All this effort, blood, sweat and tears
Must have saved them a fortune, over the years

Then there was mum, she was handy too
Just like dad, she knew a thing or two
With a hacksaw blade, she cut in half
The cupboard in the corner, next to the hearth

The Yommer was used to straighten the edges
All around the hole where there had been ledges
New wallpaper was laid...... but upside down!
But a neighbour spotted it.....and she turned it around

Road Rage

I was minding my own business, the other day
When someone thought I was in his way
He drove up fast and pulled in close
He looked quite angry and was picking his nose

He flashed his lights and honked his horn
And a pent-up frustration, was being borne
Why had he decided to pick on me?
Driving along so carefully

With too much traffic on the roads today
Road rage can occur, in this way
Bumper to bumper, toe to toe
You have to have patient......there's nowhere to go?

Come on mate, give us a break
Leave home early, then you won't be late
Better to get there all in one piece
Than risk your life......or...... get nicked by the police

The Rat Race

Life gets so busy, it passes you by
Have you ever stopped and wondered why?
So tied up in what's got to be done
We forget life is for living and having some fun

Of course there are balances, there have to be
But why so many slaves and so few free?
Is it a state of mind we are conditioned with?
As our days slip by, like sand through a sieve

Do we make ourselves busy, because we can't relax?
Is it that simple, or are there other facts?
Maybe it's time to think things through
Maybe it's time to have a minute or two

Life just goes on, I hear you say
But what is the quality, the price you pay?
Living your life, all work and no play
You're caught in a rat race...... that will kill you one day

The Snack Pack Box

The snack pack box looks such a delight
It's the only food going, on our homeward flight
The brochure describes it as a delicious treat
With a variety of food stuff for you to eat

There's tea, coffee, hot chocolate and booze
Again there's plenty for you to choose
Then they arrive, on the Dolly Trolley
Pushed by a stewardess who seems in a hurry!

The drinks are delivered, the snacks come next
But the price for the size has everyone vex
The snack pack picture, was a hamper full
But the box delivered is tiny and dull

Cries of rip-off and similar are protested
But we give in to hunger as they're digested
Our time soon passes on this two and a half hour flight
So everything considered...... it serves us right!!!

Common Sense

Close your eyes, breathe in and feel
What your senses experience, what is real
Sight alone can miss what is there
Sometimes you don't see...even through a stare

Then there are sounds that conjure a vision
But those alone may cause confusion
Maybe a smell that's in the air
Can detect that something...you think is there

Touch alone, sensed through the skin
Can mislead the information you feel within
Last but not least is the taste of it all
But that alone can confuse what you recall

Individual senses can be hard to analyse
But used together we rationalise
The five common senses...sight, hearing, smell, taste and touch
But there is a sixth...that we rely on so much!!

Date, Set And Match

The date was set, the guest's were invited
All that remained...... was to get them united
He wore a sleek pin-striped suit
Her wedding dress, had a modern look

The bride was conveyed in a smart white car
Completing a journey they had been longing for
Eloquently attired, she nervously arrived
Hoping the Groom, had also survived

Trembling with anticipation and veins in full strain
His heart was racing like a train
Then she appeared...... beautiful...... serene
The woman he loved, his perfect dream

By the look in their eyes, love was here
And everyone present, wiped his tear
Vows were exchanged...... she promised to be his trout
He sealed the occasion by exclaiming..........

"Without-a-doubt"

A & Eeyore

A recent throat infection caused my airway to close in spasm. This meant that I would be suddenly deprived of air for about thirty seconds or so. As you can imagine this was very distressing, not only for me, but for others who stood helplessly by. All forms of medication offered by my doctor failed to resolve the problem which began to get worryingly worse. Alarmed by the symptoms I attended my local hospital to be casually told there was nothing wrong with me. After a couple of visits to the A & E department I was referred to a specialist and the matter was later resolved.

My symptoms arrived quickly and I was in distress
I had a bad virus, on my chest
Coughing and choking with no airways clear
I thought asphyxia was certain, or very near

Very few options were open to me
So I went to my local A & E
I took my bag, expecting to stay
But after a check up, I was turned away

My tests proved clear and I wasn't believed
So they politely asked me to take my leave
One week later and still suffering the attacks
I returned to hospital, so they could re-check their facts

New tests were done, but nothing had changed
The doctor was stumped. "Nothing here to be gained"
She said, "No further tests can be done for you
I've done the best that I can do"

So that was it, they said nothing could be done
I was angry and frustrated with everyone
My symptoms were unknown and obviously rare
But the fact remained my asphyxia was there

Cheerfully smiling the doctor then said .....
You won't stop breathing or end up dead
These symptoms are completely unknown to us
So kindly get dressed and stop making a fuss

I left the hospital in total despair
With my original illness still blatantly there
Don't worry about me I won't go back anymore
You should rename your department 'A & Eeyore.'

The Book Signing

*I went shopping in Bolton Town Centre with my partner Janet.
We were scouting for Christmas presents and after due
deliberation I decided on a few items of clothes to buy. Now they
say women are bad at shopping, but I am unbearable. I seem to
take forever and even then after trying on everything in the shop I
might walk away with just one item. This occasion was no
different from any other and the poor girl was exhausted at the
end of it all.*

*On the way back to the car I visited one of the large book stores
for a 'mooch' around. Whilst there, I found out that Tracy
Dawson was visiting the store, to sign her recently published
book of Les' scripts and comic sketches. Because she was caught
up in traffic we decided to finish off our shopping and return for
the signing later. Then things went array:*

It was one of those days; I was invited to shop
My partner's determination, I couldn't stop
Christmas was approaching, presents too buy
Excuses don't work, so don't even try

So we got in the car and drove to the stores
Parked in the car park and secured the doors
I was asked for clues as to what she could buy me
I had no idea and said "nothing.... really"

We walked into the mall and began to look
That's when it hit me, I needed this book
She raised her eyes, huffed and puffed at that
And suggested I put on my thinking cap

I decided on jeans and training shoes
So she left me in the store and I started to browse
I tried things on for over an hour
She was getting desperate, becoming quite dower

Never before had she met a bloke like me
So annoying.... so bloody fussy!
The problem I have, is my clothes have to feel right
When I think I'm finished, I usually catch sight

Of something I missed that looks real cool
So it's back to the changing rooms....she now needs a stool
At last I finish, garments paid for and packed
She looks kind of weary....sort of whacked
The book store was next, even though she was waning
Authors were there. They had books for signing
So I chatted to one and was having fun
Put both bags down and picked up one

On leaving the store she stopped and exclaimed
"The other bag.... you've left it behind"
I quickly returned, the bag was still there
Near to the table, down by the chair

One of the authors was running late
Stuck in traffic, but still making the date
More shopping done we returned...plus a table
Placing them down, I was then quite able

To rest my bags and take up a stance
And receive my book, signed with thanks
"At last" she said, as we made down the stair
Then suddenly stopped and cried out in despair

"Give me those bags and return to the room.
The table is missing you have left it buffoon"
Hysterically laughing, no more could be said
"Men when shopping are completely brain dead"

Wedding Vows

After great thought and much a-do
Vows for the wedding were prepared for the two
Each had their own to convey to the other
Alarmingly simple and not too much bother

He promised to love, honour and obey
In a manner befitting the mood of the day
She promised to love and honour as well
But, if he dares to cross her, she'll give him hell

Then the clause; a get me out
Slipped in by both, in case of doubt
A renewable contract, every three year
Well she said, it's what we do with the car

He wanted more; like his agent had said
Forget your genitals and think with your head
You don't turn out and give your all
If the management's going...... to take away your ball

The Grand National

The Grand National, is an annual treat
  Where a nation bet's on galloping feet
Any horse can win, as they jokey for the line
Striving for position and glory time

Is there a system, for choosing the one?
Do you study form...... like' the rule of thumb'
Do you pick a name, or consult mystic Meg?
Or stab at the paper with a lucky peg

Each way, or on the nose!
How will you bet, in this greatest of shows?
Punters and owners grit their teeth and pray
But whatever the method, its luck on the day

A hero in the making, a champion today
A place in history, come what may
Fortunes to be made and fortunes lost
But the adrenalin rush is worth the cost

Road Trip

A date's been set, the road trip's on
Come this Wednesday, both will have gone
Off to Spain with an open ticket
Will they stay or return. Will they risk it?

A caravan awaits our adventurous two
The Omega diaries, will record what they do
Travel to Southampton then bed and float
Its fifteen hundred miles by road and boat

At journeys end, the caravan awaits?
The customised version, could sell tea and cakes?
The odd bacon butty and cup of char
Would go down nicely in their makeshift bar

If not a bar then maybe a hotel
Will they convert it, only time will tell?
I hope to see Dave and Roe again?
But If I don't...... the sun's to blame

MS Braemar

MS Braemar the Olsen Line ship
Was made a little longer, by adding an extra bit
Now two hundred more, can sleep in her bow
No staff increase...... but they manage somehow

The cabins are nice, compact and clean
But not the best that we have seen
Paul the waiter, is a dancing queen
He is the campest barman you have ever seen

Princess KK, short for King Kong
Is the Bar Deck charmer, with a memory, so ooooooh long?
They work so hard, over many hours
With a little time off during our tours

A luxury holiday...... at a bargain price
If only the Ports could be as nice
So bon voyage' to you and everyone
Let's hope we meet again...... on the next one

The Brotherhood

It's often said, tongue in cheek
Men are strong and women are weak
Let's discuss this old cliché
And examine the facts that exist today

The truth we find is just the opposite
Women have power...... We only front it
Things have changed, since days of old
Now men are manipulated and do as they're told

We are like...... a brotherhood
Who'd change things back...... if we could!
Some men will deny it, so it seems
Are they right? In your dreams

Open your eyes and realise
Women are cunning, control, and devise
Don't kid yourself, or you'll be in bother
And you'll be denied...... 'A bit of the other'

Four Eyes

It disappears before your eyes
Your clarity of vision is in demise
A fact for certain, you cannot deny
As the ageing process, slips on by

Objects and letters have become slightly blurred
But you won't admit it, it's quite absurd
Will wearing glasses be like losing your hair?
Will people look at me, stand and stare?

Long sighted, short sighted, whatever it be
Why has this suddenly happened to me?
An eye sight test will clearly reveal
The glasses you need and the cost of the deal

Then you remember, all those jokes and teases
To all the people you pulled to pieces
Now you've become one of those guys
How do you like it? .... 'Four eyes'

Dufercating Nurkeler

The Dufercating Nurkeler
Has such an elegant sound
It's a word used for everything
When the proper one can't be found

Where did this word come from?
I don't know...... do you?
Everyone seems to use it
When they are stuck for a word or two

This word is an ally
A friend, when needed most
Don't forget to use it
When your brain has given up the ghost

You won't find it in the dictionary
So don't go and look in there
It's not in the thesaurus either
Because it's not written down anywhere!

The Christmas List

Christmas approaches, excitement abounds
Parents are struggling with no money around
Finances are tight, we are feeling the squeeze
Keep it simple kids. Please! Please! Please!

No big demands will be met this year?
I've had a whisper in Santa's ear
Only one toy on Christmas day
Will be delivered to you from Santa's slay

It's no good arguing, puffing or panting?
That's the situation, regardless of the ranting?
Toys from last year, are still unpacked?
They created a mountain, they were so highly stacked

Christmas will be merry and full of good cheer
With plenty of room to move this year
Your toy is so special. It's a buy one, get one free
After it's unpacked; play with the box...... you do it annually!!

It's Raining (Again)

The sky is full, the clouds are black
The weather's not cutting us any slack
It's supposed to be summer wearing a smile
What do we get? Water, by the mile

Our national grid is overflowing
So much water keeps pouring and pouring
We get some respite now and again
But on the whole it's just the same

Deserted and forgotten our land is in gloom
The false tan industry is having a boom
Come on sun; pay us a visit
A few warm rays would be exquisite

I'm sorry if our winds are too cold for you
And turn your rays a shivering blue
Come back please, it's just not fair
Everyone else is getting our share

Size Isn't Everything!

I haven't put weight on, my pants have shrunk
My shirt isn't tight, I have a large trunk

My skin isn't baggy, it just looks slack
I have a clip, to hold it all back

I'm not small, if I stand on my toes
But I have a big heart, as everyone knows

I am a specimen of the weirdest kind
But a diamond for sure, this you'll find

I believe the emphasis must surely be
Don't look on the surface or at what you see

It's the person within that holds the key
And he's enormous, I guarantee

The Secret Door

I have a secret door?
It takes me to places I can explore
Completely hidden, like the dead of night
Inside my bedroom, out of sight

Whilst lost in thought sat on my bed
With new adventures inside my head
I suddenly envisage a magical door
That appears from nowhere in my bedroom floor

It looks all wobbly and is ever so bright.
And emits a hazy, shimmering light
I was scared, yet excited, with surprise on my face
What adventures await me, in this magical place?

I ventured inside and took a chance
I fought aliens and dragons, and shunned romance
My distant travels and adventurous tales
Are full of excitement...... that never fails

Dinner Ladies

Our dinner ladies are a motley crew
Dedicated to the job they like to do
Full time mums working their fingers to the bone
Fitting in school, as well as home

Every day's a battle to try and feed the kid's
With swinging spatulas and dripping sieves
Preparing school meals, is an art, a craft
It also entails a lot of graft

The kids will moan and groan at that
But the food is magic, pulled out of a hat
They conjure up dinners at a very low cost
Ensuring vitamins and nutrients never get lost

Noisy, sweaty, and full of stains
Their uniforms are splattered, with food remains
Enough of the kids!! .... What about the cooks?
They're good enough to eat, with those dishy looks

Pompeii

In 79 AD she awoke, having slept
Ten miles too town she quietly crept
As the silence rained down, the message was complete
The 17 year promise, was hers to keep

Vesuvius had spoken during the midst of day
And no-one could stop her having her say
For those that remained no mercy was shown
Preserved for posterity in an ash covered gown

They lay entombed until 1738
Until Pompeii was uncovered...... as they began to excavate
Death had come knocking at their door
Not for the last time you can be assured

The Optimistic Pessimist

I'm as certain about this, as anyone can be
Disaster awaits me, just wait and see
I'm not a worrier; well not any more... But!
You never know what knocks at your door

A positive outlook is all I need
The kind of thinking that's guaranteed
To see me through the toughest of day's... But!
Disaster can strike in so many ways

Things will be alright on the day?
Well maybe sometimes, don't quote me, ok
No sense worrying, it may never happen ... But!
Maybe it will, what do you reckon?

Be optimistic see the bright side of life
Pessimists worry, about all the gloom and strife
Life can be richer, balanced between the two... But!
I'm not sure. What about you?

The Dentist's Chair

It started with a niggle, a wince and then an ache
The throbbing in my tooth was too much to take
So I telephoned the dentist and booked a slot
Come on Monday, was the response I got

Three days later I found myself there
And was fully examined in the dentist chair
"I can see the one" he told me straight
I'll take an x-ray and look at the plate

The infection confirmed, I was given pills to cure
I then paid my money and was shown the door
"If it still persists I'll whip it out
With a tooth like that I can't afford to mess about"

So a week later I was back in the chair
To rid myself of the tooth in despair
A quick examination proved the dentist right
I had one to come out and another in plight

A jab in the gums and a wait in reception
Prepared me for, my tooth extraction
With a huff and a puff, and a grunt and groan
My teeth were pulled out and then I went home

No more pain now the teeth have gone
But I really wish, it had only been one.
The rest are sparkling, neat and clean
The very best half set that's ever been seen

The Two Desperados

This story originated after a marathon shopping expedition.
The two culprits shall remain nameless, but they know who
they are. They went out to blitz the shops early one morning
and returned late in the afternoon exhausted. Their purses
were empty, their bags were full, but maybe the food
shopping had been too dull?

They ventured out on a mission impossible
A dynamic duo quite unstoppable
Their aim was the sales and to shop and shop
Their appetites wetted, they just couldn't stop

Their stead was a stallion in the form of a car
No distance unreachable, near or far
Fired up and ready to go
Her foot hit the pedal, "do you know the meaning of slow"

Two desperados armed to the hilt
Both bearing credit cards; blood could be spilt
Look out Bolton here they come
The siege of the stores had just begun

Once in town the rampage began
Every store targeted; none were shun
Weary and weak after days of clothes shopping
They return to their lair to rest after stopping

Perusing their goods they felt a glow inside
The shopping had gone well, but were they satisfied?
They looked at each other with a quizzical grin
Then they remembered.... they had no food in.

The Chocoholic

A rush of desire floods her brain
The box of chocolates, is in her head again
Teasing thoughts pass through her mind
Shall I open it? What will I find?

The chocolates were located on the top shelf
Maybe just one, to treat myself
Looking around to plot her route
She quickly rises and with light of foot

Makes her way there with a quickened pace
Her juices are flowing, she's a total disgrace
She tells herself, what a pleasure this will be
To eat one or two whilst watching TV

But once at the cupboard, the temptation is too much
She tears the box open and scoops six with one clutch
Quickly she returns and sits in her chair
To satisfy the craving and ease her despair

Her taste buds tingle, as she nibbles the tit-bits
She knows this is going...... 'straight on the hips'
She eats one, then two, and drifts off into heaven
Full of remorse, she thinks to herself.... I should have had seven

The Magic Bushes

*Playing Hide and Seek with my son and his friend on
the local park developed into a monster game. They
loved the idea of a monster lying in wait for them
hidden in the bushes. No prizes for guessing who
played the monster. We called them the magic bushes.*

L ook out kids! He's hiding in there
Inside the bushes, just waiting to scare
That's where he dwell's, hidden from sight
Creeping out, during day and night

His teeth are yellow and his gums are green
I suspect they never have been clean
His eyes are narrow and his lips are thin
He is grumpy and moody and twenty feet ten

His arms are long when he stretches them out
And his voice is so loud he doesn't have to shout
You can try and hide but it's a hopeless task
No-one escapes, you need only ask

Enter the magic bushes at your own risk
If you do, you will be sadly missed
Rumour has it, he eats everyone
So avoid the menu, he likes kids well done.

Rosie Lee

There's nothing better than a nice cup of tea
Brewed in the pot, the perfect Rosie Lee

It's the taste that's so special, a comforting treat
That allows you to relax and put up your feet

The choice of leaf, gets the taste is just right
Boiling water infuses, making a brewing delight

Accompaniments are varied, lemon and milk are just two
It's your personal choice that makes it perfect for you

Enjoyment of your cuppa doesn't stop there
The future is foretold, if you're willing to stare

At the arrangement of leaves left in your cup
But make sure they are loose, and not bagged up

The Winch Man

The Winch Man hangs by a silvery thread
Fed into danger, where no other can tread
Yet they gladly fly, where others wouldn't go
And feel the fear, without letting it show

Over the cliff tops and above the waves
How many lives have they saved?
Stranded, hurt, or caught in a swell
They face the devil and visit your hell

They aren't immortal...... flesh and bone, that's all
But in our eyes, they walk ten foot tall
So the next time you fly over land or sea
Remember these words, "Be safe for me".

Work

I remember the times my father would say
Enjoy your schooling, it soon passes away
Work hard whilst your there and don't be a clown
You will regret it forever, if you let yourself down

Knowledge is power, so keep well read
A good education puts you in good stead
As school says goodbye and it's time to leave
You prepare for the future and what to achieve

Pursue your dreams and your heart's desire
Be happy and content and you will aspire
Many choices in life, will be made by you
So enjoy your work, do the best you can do

Don't worry about choices, you can always change tack
Always look forward and never look back
Life's not mapped out or set in stone
What you reap, grows from what you have sown

Something In The Air

I've picked up a virus and my body aches
My heads now throbbing
And my coughs bang up to date

I've been to the chemist, he knows what it is
"It's something in the air"
Was his diagnosis

Some sneaky bugger has passed it on to me
By sneezing and wheezing
Without a hanky

Old sods like me have to be careful you know
We pick things up easily......!
And I'm too young to go

Couch Potato

They sit around with no movement detected
The couch potatoes, quite infected

Fixed by a TV that flashes before them
Viewing from morning past 'News at Ten'

Sometimes they stir during a commercial break
But soon return to re-partake

Sleep may occur for an hour or two
But they soon awake eager to view

At the end of the day they fall into bed
Exhausted, from viewing and totally brain dead

Me Water Bed

Oh how I love me water bed
On which I sleep each night
A watery paradise it has to be said
And it keeps me back just right

Always warm but it can be cool
The heater has a control
A conditioner inhibits mattress renewal
And there's a ballast to stop the roll

They call me the 'Capt' which comes as no shock
It's an honour they bestow on me
So even though I sleep in a dry dock
I'm always out at sea

Text Messaging

Texting has a short-hand, all of its own
Abbreviated and condensed, messages by phone
This dictation enigma, is a cursed delight
With spellings and punctuation, being contrite

Base stations transmit over land and sea
Connections occurring quite magically
Give me a clue, in this hieroglyphically quiz
English was never as double Dutch as this

My speed's getting quicker on the old key pad
But I'll always be slow, isn't that sad
If you want a reply, sooner than later
I can always send you...... 'An old fashioned letter'

My Little Note Book

I write my poems, in a little note book
Capturing the mood, on every outlook
Rhymes and verse, eloquently convey
What I feel inside and want to say

All my thoughts, unspoken
Are inspired, nurtured, and then awoken
They fall into line and are then deployed
To be read as text, interpreted and enjoyed

This place I reach into, deep inside my mind
Is a bouquet of imagination, I inhale and find
Feelings and emotions, so very key
Unique in their nature and so dear to me

The Aging Process

Moisturise and cream every day
Exercise your skin and keep those wrinkles away
What's the point? I hear you say
It's all going south......someday!

The latter of course is very true
But what's the alternative for me and you
I can be saggy under my clothes
But look at the face......and everyone knows

How kind on you, aging has been
Can depend on the make-up of your genes
Let's delay it as long as we can
There's nothing wrong with being beautiful, man

The Vatican

I tried for an audience with the Pope today
But the Vatican asked me to go away
He's chatting with god and can't be disturbed
So leave him a message......and you'll still get heard

Have a browse round if you can pay the fee
We have plenty of treasures for you to see
Don't start praying or being divine
With all this commercialism you won't have time

The crowds are so big there's nowhere to kneel
It's the money in your pocket they like to feel
Masterpieces and tapestries adorn ceiling and wall
This opulence and arrogance has been paid by us all

Aches And pains

This pain in my shoulder, it's at it again
I've had it so long, I've forgot the medical name
From the moment I wake, to the moment I sleep
You can hear me coming by the sound of the creak

Some say I deserve it..... It's the cross I bear
But I think its old age, just wear and tear
So I live with it...... as you do!
So what kind of pain is troubling you?

George The Cat

It's ten o'clock and the door slams shut
George arrives home oh what luck
Too cautious to wander from his domain
He peeps around the corner, then back again

Day one passes slowly and George cannot be found
Is he down by the stereo or somewhere else around?
There is food on the floor and water to drink
But George is not for eating, he is sulking I think

By the end of the week he is a different fellow
No longer shy, timid or mellow
He owns the house and he lets it show
He is a cat in a million and we love him so

He is ever so gorgeous and a bit of a lad
Two men in the house and he's the lad
I have another love, but she will have to share
The big Tabby Cat, with the orange hair

Rita The Chameleon

Three layers of clothing at least each day
Can be shed from her body in a Chameleon display
As the temperature drops or takes a rise
The transition occurs before your eyes

Rita the Chameleon is our Italian guide
Who ensures her tourists are satisfied
No task too great, no deed too small
Rita is the one who looks after us all

Riding shot gun at Javier's side
She shoots out information, in a verbal tirade
She loves her job with a passion
The Archers tour op, with her own style of fashion

The Yearning

It started with thoughts about what used to be
How she used to laugh and feel so...... happy
Alone at home, evening stretched into night
And a yearning inside her, started to bite

Times were relived...... the good and the bad
Boy, those good times, were the best she ever had
The bad are buried, in a place locked away
Where they cannot harm her; well that's what she'll say

Loneliness preys. It's stark and real
This in reality, is how millions feel
Trapped with no hope of breaking free
The telephone's a life line...... company

Don't live in the past, or let it drag you down
Life is for living, turn it around
Wear a smile, sing a happy tune
Life is much brighter, viewed from a sunny room

Sky Line

The sky was full. It was an awesome sight
Huge clouds gathered, hung in flight
Their power and glory were stunning to see
Colossal formations, gigantic to me

The colours were bland, yet an elegant blue-grey and white
The largest one, as deep as the night
Hypnotically floating, it held me in awe
Nature's creation, laid out raw

The weather was fine but had a promise in bloom
As the sun tried in vain to disperse the gloom
The master painter had mixed and crafted
A sky brushed out and perfectly drafted

Night And Day

The sun sits low this summer night
Skirting the tree tops, with a dazzling light
It's off to lands and pastures new
Places hidden from our view

As our night falls, to their day break
We lower our heads as they awake
Our day is rested as theirs begins
This is the process of nature's whims

With deserts to heat and grasslands to dry
The sun gently rises into their sky
Earth's angle of deviation, is a 2 degree tilt
That spins our world, without anything being spilt

Tranquillity

As I sit, a quiet stillness settles about
The mantle clock ticks, with a quiet shout
I hear noises...... usually hidden
Then I relax, and experience the forbidden

The house has its own interminable way
Creaking and groaning, like the old man of its day
I close my eyes and just feel the mood
This is a time to which I allude

Moments, when nothing needs to be done
A special time, for everyone
Empower yourself. Let body and mind be in sync
Take the time to stop, relax, and think

My Valentine

Oh Valentine, what can I say
You have me smiling every day
You are the perfect partner, lover and mate
A beautiful creation, there can be no mistake

Every touch, every feeling, every beat of my heart
Every movement, every breath, underwritten by Mozart
A symphony of feelings, so much give and take
Cementing a union, no one can break

So when all those around us, are trying so hard
With gifts and hollow sentiments, we gladly discard
These things we both know are clearly certain
Together we are drawn, until the final curtain

My perfect woman, is embodied in you
Love has found me, this is true
Drawn us together, so naturally
A love like ours, will last for eternity

Election Day

Going to vote for myself, this year
I'm the only one that seems to care
Are we underfoot, or just in the way
Struggling on from day to day

Crimes on the increase, but they tell you not
The money in your pocket isn't worth a lot
My jobs not safe…that could soon go
And I worry a lot, without letting it show

Our kids are educated to the hilt
With nowhere to go, in this society we have built
I don't like moaning but enough is enough
This good life isn't coming…and each year is tough

I 'm getting elected, looking after number one
Pocketing some wealth, for me and my son
I will do…whatever it takes
Then at least I'll be responsible…for my own mistakes.

The Big 'C'

Where does it all begin?
On the surface, or deep within
The big 'C' time bomb hidden from sight
Waiting to explode when the time is right

No-one is immune, or so it seems
Young or old, or in your teens
Will it strike in you or me?
I don't know, we will wait and see

We learn every day how to put things right
Every day we continue to fight the fight
Could it be our environmental upbringing?
Is it smoking, drinking, or what we are eating?

I don't know; what do you think or say?
We live along side it every day
We live our lives as we choose
Health is a lottery you either win or lose

Secrets

Never reveal your secrets
I don't care what they are
We try and hide them
But we wear them like a scar

Never reveal your secrets
Then only you will know
What your heart is withholding
And what lies below

Never reveal your secrets
Keep them all locked away
Secrets can only be shared
If you chance them surfacing one day

Never reveal your secrets
Take them to the grave
Never, ever, reveal your secrets
Or there is a price to be paid

Ann Summers

Our Ann Summers meetings are full of party tricks
They have sexy underwear to titillate those naughty bits

Little toys that tickle and tease
For you and your partner, hoping to please

There is the Tease Spanker and Door Jam Cuffs
The Cheeky Monkey Pouches and a load of unmentionable stuff

You put them here, you put them there
In fact, you can put them anywhere

However, don't poke or prod where there is a no entry sign
Get permission, or face a fine.

The Simulator Production

The boys disappeared upstairs out of view
'They had a certain something'...... they wanted to do
So I left them alone and they developed an idea
A simulator production...... for me to hear

When they were ready, I was called upstairs
The lights were dimmed and the moment was theirs
One performed; the other, a special effects man
Shone a torch at the window, whilst the performance
began

Silhouetted castles, war and space travel
A fascinating story began to unravel
How lucky I am to have shared with them
The simulator experience......which scored, ten out of ten

The Sun Bed

L aid out in lines under the sun
Umbrella's and sun beds stretch out a welcome
There for your use, throughout the day
To provide shade and comfort...... in every way

Two positions are offered by the bed mechanism
Lying or sitting it's your decision
Then there's a sun screen, attached to the bed
To pin-point shade...... for your face or head

Attached by a line they can be circled around
To catch the sun as it turns without sound
From this position you could be forgiven
For thinking you had arrived......on a beach, in heaven

Mind Games

It's my memory you see
It lets me down, continually

To some it's a curse, me losing my mind
But to me it's a blessing, I think you'll find

When those around me are stressed and hurried
I casually plod on, totally unworried

Every act, or deed, a fresh challenge anew
Unlike the world, that troubles you

Don't worry about me, or start to fret
Because I can't remember, all the things I forget!!

The Lupanari

Strategically positioned around old Pompeii
The' Lupanari' opens night and day
These are the rooms offering a 'personal touch'
With men paying handsomely, no matter how much

Phallic street signs carve the way
With manly shapes up on display
Some are in the roadway pointing too
Just so you know which streets to walk through

Pompeii had everything and even more
It was a sea port haven, visitors loved to explore
Nothing has changed over the years
We now pay our respect, and shed our tears

The Taxi Mash

Sunday night, and nothing's new
Sat on the rank, feeling blue
The jobs have dried up, just for a while
We are waiting for the rush, to get us mobile

Kicking our heels and waiting to cruise!
The rank quartet, play the blues
No ivories to tickle, or Sax to play
But harmonies erupt as the cabs start to sway

Horns begin crooning and headlamps flash
As the cars go crazy doing the 'taxi mash'
Its infectious rhythms can't be forgot
Playing the blues, certainly hits the spot

Calendar Girl

B e my calendar girl, make my dreams come true
With a pose for each month, only of you
You have a figure to die for and the look of a queen
We will create a masterpiece, never before seen

From January to December I will capture every pose
Your curvaceous displays will abandon those clothes
But I'm dreaming of course, these things will never be
Next year if you're lucky you can have one of me

The Visitor

Peter the rabbit had a visitor today
A cat called Thomas came to play
Thomas thought Peter was a white kangaroo
Hopping around in shoe size 22

Now that's pretty big if you have little paws
So the first sight of Peter caused him to pause
He wasn't frightened, he just stood and gazed
At the big fluffy rabbit, completely amazed

Thomas jumped down off the garden fence
And sat with Peter who didn't take offence
They chatted a while in the heat of the sun
Then Thomas had to leave, he had to run

The time for food had laid its claim
As Thomas felt hungry and Peter the same
So they made a date for another day
When Thomas had time to come and play

Flight Of Fancy

When love flies out of the window
And your mind slams shut the door
Emotions are jaded!
You can't take it any more

The embers that were burning
Now smoulder with no flame
Release me from this oppression
I need to breathe again

Fighting to the surface
Drowning in dismay
I tried so hard to fix it
But love wasn't here to stay

Thoughts Of You

It's, one o'clock and I just can't sleep
I close my eyes and in you creep

Your presence is felt even though you're not there
I can smell your perfume, even touch your hair

I sense your body, so warm to the touch
Your legs entwine me I want you so much

My heart starts racing; I am lost in a trance
I dream of love making in this perfect romance

Gently my darling, hold me tight
Squeeze me, stroke me, this feels so right

We are lovers in love, our hearts beat together
We shall keep it this way forever and ever

Jack

It was August, way back in 1888
The nights were long, and as dark as slate
The air was still, and not a breath spoke
As time ticked by, with a deathly stroke

The fire in his head was burning bright
His mood was dangerous, the chemistry in flight
His hand reached out, then took her life
The rest was horrible as he used his knife

The rage was uncontrollable, the intention no mistake
Her life was taken, as if his to take
Now in denial, the rage all gone
She was left all alone; lifeless; a pattern had begun

Who was the monster in White Chapel at night?
Named Jack the ripper, because "what he done weren't right"
More lives would be claimed before he was gone
But they never found out, where he had came from

The Leaf

Delicately balanced on the tree
The leaf starts to bud, its spring you see
From bud to leaf and then to flower
New born life, unfolds this hour

Natures cycle, again on tour
Summers approaching, everything in flower
Dancing and swaying in the breeze
Music voiced, in the trees

Autumn comes. Then, all yellow and brown
Not long now, before they carpet the ground
The seasons are changing and winters here
The leaves so crisp, then they disappear

Winter arrives, the trees are stripped bare
Everything gone, except the evergreen stare
Everything sleeping, everything on hold
The air is biting, everywhere cold

Twins

Born together and perfectly matched
Uniquely formed and totally detached

Their position in life always has them on view
But the way you have kept them, is a credit to you

The passage of time has not taken its toll
Equals in life, they are twins that's all

Defying gravity they stand so proud
Two's company, three's not allowed

Winds of Change

The force of nature is an awesome thing
The wind stings the trees and makes them sing
Branches bend, trees are uprooted
Buildings get damaged, her temper is vented

The sea is swelling, everything in change
Temperatures soaring, the planets in rage
Is nature deciding, does she have a choice?
Is our interference, something to rejoice?

Can global warming be blamed for it all?
Is our responsibility, great or small?
We occupy the planet, as the dominant race
The way we have treated it, is a total disgrace

So when she punishes us, in her own interminable way
It's a way of saying you've had your day
When mankind has gone and been removed without trace
Will the world evolve into a better place?

Learning Curve

New social networking tools and techniques
Convey information within days not weeks
This transmission......from one, too the other
Occurs without complication, or too much bother

Classroom boredom will be a thing of the past
Now we are shown, simply and fast
Classroom rhetoric was once quite hip
Now it's replaced by the silicone chip

Electronic learning leads the way
This effective tool is here to stay
So instead of 20% staying in
There's more for the brain......than the recycled bin

Night Walker

A s night rests its head and dawn cracks a smile
Sleep surrenders to utter beguile
My body is restless and my minds in flow
I have to get up.......but there's nowhere to go

I journey to the kitchen in the middle of the night
Where demons and shadows are hidden within sight
I join them for company and sit alone
As the stillness of night, settles about my home

I am a night walker, pacing the floor at night
With a mind that's burning, without respite
Yes, sleep for me, would be heaven
But I keep on dreaming, twenty four seven

Depression

Funny thing this depression
The way it grinds you down
Every day is a battle; a smile warring frown

Others can't understand it
This darkness that glows within
I'm slowly going under; because I can't swim

I don't mean to be moody.
My chemistry just ebbs and flows
Can somebody please help me; god only knows

Time

When our time finishes, will eternity end?
In a Universe expanding, so infinite to comprehend
Everything balanced, turning in sync
When you ponder this phenomenon, it's hard to think

Where will this journey take us too?
Will there be other dimensions to view?
Seconds pass freely, but are they lost?
Our lives are lived, but at what cost?

Will our souls meet up with those who have gone?
Will we be reunited, with everyone?
What's in store, will we eventually see?
When time no longer matters, for you and me

A Nip In The Air

It's so cold outside, the air bites at your skin
The day finally surrenders, to a battle it cannot win
Icy winds busying themselves, here and there
And the temperature drops with a Mercury scare

Quietly the frost veils the ground
Idyllically falling all around
A dusting of white sets the scene
Broken by footprints where people have been

Night has fallen, people now sleep
Tucked up in their beds where no cold can creep
When they awake, will they cherish the day?
Or curse under their breaths, asking it to go away

The Merry-Go-Round

L ife is a mystery, as if you didn't know
A game of cards with no hand to show
A merry-go-round with twists and turns
Some say its balanced and giving earns

Others just take and nothing is bought
Selfish actions, made without thought
Turning the page of each precious day
Destiny leads us along our way

Are we in control of what we do?
Do my actions...... also affect you?
Is the path we walk, the one we choose?
Sometimes we win and sometimes we lose

As the cycle of life, turns its great wheel
We destroy each other by the anger we feel
Are we freaks of nature that fell into place?
Was the world created...... for the human race?

Misunderstood

All men are equal...... now that's a joke!!!
There's no such a thing...... as Mr average bloke
One common thought! ...... We all think the same
Evolutionary players; playing the game

That simple trait, inherited by all
Womanising! Our greatest downfall
We see hunter, turning carer, confusing the two
A difficult balance, we find hard to pursue

Women don't understand us ...... they just don't see
How sensitive we are, full of complexity
Occasionally untidy, in this hell of a zoo
We multi task just to satisfy you

So the next time you say, "Men are all the same"
Think again and try to refrain
From putting us, all in the same boat
Because we're treading water...... trying to keep afloat

The Masochist

Cheese and chocolate are the triggers for me
A lethal combination, I can guarantee
Add a drop of red wine, which I love to devour
And it'll deliver a migraine, within the hour

For me...... that's a headache from hell
With speech impairment, nausea and dizziness as well
If you heed the warnings, you can avoid an attack
But thicko's like me keep going back

It's not that I'm stupid and I'm no masochist
I just satisfy my cravings, which I can't resist
I know when I'm eating...... what to expect
So when I'm ill, I get no respect

"I told you so! ...... It's your own silly fault"
Is the sympathetic tirade she'll exalt?
So I wash the pills down and ride the pain
"Cheers".
Here's to the next time...... when I try them again!!

Turkey Trot

I was driving down the motorway
When a Turkey passed me by
It was powered by three legs
And refusing to fly

I followed with haste
Barely keeping it in my sight
As the bird began to accelerate
Pushing on with all its might

After about five miles
It suddenly veered left
So I followed behind
Putting my skills to the test

Down country roads
Then into a farm
It disappeared out of sight
Taking refuge in a barn

I came across the farmer
Who saw my look of surprise
His smile was broad and canny
And he had a twinkle in his eyes

In response to my question
About the three legged bird
He told me he bred them
Because he needed a third

I said, "What do they taste like?"
Are they tender after such a run?
He said, "I'll let you know...... If I ever catch one"

The Manual

I don't care how good a DIY person you are, but even the best of you have come across the construction manual from hell. They are usually written in several languages, except the one of clarity and common sense. Many manuals have given up on supplying a written explanation and now just provide explanatory pictures in assembly order. That's probably because none of us read them anyway!! Unfortunately, even the pictures are confusing. To be fair, the diagrams are quite good. It's just that the panels that come flat packed can't be identified until you have assembled them, usually upside down!!

Written for self assembly
So that you can easily construct
Flat packed products
Without getting yourself wound up......!!

Falling under the heading
'D.I.Y'
The frustrations of 'The Manual'
Will make you cry

After an hour or so
I feel kind of queasy
Reading these instructions
Should be......so easy!!

Then!!
The ultimate let me down
A screw won't fit......
It's square, not round

Upside down
This way, then that!!
You'll need training
In unarmed combat

Finally together!!
The jobs now stopped
But the wardrobes turned cupboard
After parts were lopped

Question & Answer

Q: Do you love me?
A: With all my heart
Q: How long will you love me?
A: Forever, my sweetheart

Q: Will you always adore me?
A: Until the end of time
Q: Will you always want me?
A: Like a verse requires a rhyme

Q: Will we always be together?
A: I don't know, one can never say!
Q: Do you intend to leave me?
A: I will, if you carry on this way

Q: What does our love, mean to you?
A: You're beginning to fry my brain
Q: You never tell me you love me?
A: I do...... time and time again

Q: Do we have problem?
A: Only you badgering me so
Q: But I only want to love you......?
A: I know...... that's why I must go

Battle Cry

We hear how bravely they have fallen
In the name of some heroic cause
But that's no consolation
For fighting another's wars

Of course we need defending
If our shores are under attack
But what's the point of sending
Our hero's to a foreign outback

When we're fighting another's battle
Faraway from our shores
Let's concentrate on our survival
Now that's an honourable cause

All great empires have fallen
History, links us with them all
Yet we still harbour this illusion
We're everyone's defender...... itching for a brawl

Oscar

Oscar has a new family
He is only ten weeks old
Bought from the kennels this Saturday
He is handsome, cute and bold

His coat is black and furry
As woolly as a lamb
This Scotty dog is a treasure
Learning the ropes as best he can

Toilet training is essential
But he can't use it like we do
That's not doggy possible
As he keeps falling down the hole in the loo

So he uses the mat in the kitchen
As a temporary measure.......a start!
If only he could stop using topspin
Because he keeps missing the mark

The Diary

*One of the presents I received for my fifteenth birthday was a
five year diary. As I flicked through the empty pages, I tried to
imagine what the future had in store for me. Five years seemed
so far off and for some inexplicable reason I recall wondering
what the world might be like when I was fifty. Of course I had
no idea how things were going to unfold, but it was a strange
moment nonetheless. This is a short poem about that moment.*

I was only fifteen
When I received 'The Diary', with a five year ream
It had a locking clasp and was leather bound
A present off an Aunt, who was short and round

It was 1965, a new age hour
Mod's and Rockers...... Hippies and flower power
Mod's clashed with Rockers on the beach
Hippies flocked to communes, with free love to preach

Five long years lay ahead?
What route would be taken......What path would I tread?
All of life's secrets still tucked up in bed
If chronicled...... would they later be read?

I remember sitting quietly, thumbing each empty page
Pondering life's challenge at each and every stage
Now I'm in my fifties and time has trundled by
I still remember that diary...... left blank so no-one could pry!!

The Manoeuvre

I'm watching a lady trying to park her car
She's in reverse and not going very far
Trying to manoeuvre into a parking bay
The car keeps turning, this and that way

It should be as simple as A, B, C
She's in a panic...... having a calamity
Use your mirrors, keep watching your back?
The cars either side, think they're under attack

So it's forward again, to straighten her line
Is she going to do it...... this or next time?
I doubt very much if there's any chance of that
She couldn't reverse into the Watford Gap

Finally exhausted and still not parked
She's red in the face and looking narked
No energy for shopping after this marathon
Oh, isn't reversing...... impossible for some!!

Sods Law

Just when you think it can't get any worse,
Disaster strikes......Totally unrehearsed
You're trying to avoid putting yourself on view
When the opposite happens and the spotlights on you

Being caught out means there's nowhere to hide
Your credibility's in tatters with a dent in your pride
Scurrying away hoping for damage limitation
There's very little chance of saving the situation

It's Sods Law, you were well caught out.
No point worrying or trying to shout
Take it on the chin...... laugh it off
Taking 'yourself' to seriously, is pretty dull stuff

The Hypochondriac

S wathed in bandages from head to toe
That cut on my finger could go septic you know
I'm not really touting for any attention
It's a guard against certain, imminent infection

Prevention is better than cure, I've always said
Remember what happened to poor old Uncle Fred
He went into hospital after a coughing bout
Popped his clogs and never came out

You can never be too careful in this day and age
A runny nose can go on the rampage
Before you know it, the common cold
Has become an epidemic, killing young and old

I was surfing the internet the other day
And couldn't believe all the ailments on display
I've had most; if not all; of those medical terms
If I wasn't so ill......I'd do a Masters in germs

"Without-A-Doubt
In-Order And
Happy Days"

*We all have quirky sayings for one thing or another and these can change
or vary from time to time. I was using 'in-order' quite a lot, to make a point
or emphasise agreement with something someone might be saying. I struck
up a friendship with two great guys who visited my local hostillery. I soon
realised that they had their own unique words for emphasising their
agreement when engaged in, or listening to someone else's conversation. We
quite innocently fell into a rhythm of using our sayings and it developed into
quite a funny routine. We still fall into this even after long spells of not
seeing each other.*

They called themselves, 'Without-a-doubt, In-order and Happy Days
'Three drinking buddies, with humorous way's
Without-a-doubt was short and slim
Adorning a smile from ear to chin

In-order, was the older of the crew
A steadying influence on the other two
Happy days was chirpy and bright
A team leader with goals in sight

The three teamed up in their local pub
Becoming regulars......as you would
Conversations were concluded with these three cliché's

Without-a-doubt!
    In-order!
        Happy days!